For our ancestors.

CONTENTS

ACKNOWLEDGMENTS

Thank you to my mom for her faith, love, and support especially through these tough few years post-dad. I don't have enough words to express my gratefulness. She is the reason I know that God exists.
- Liz Matory

I would like to thank my grandfather JC for teaching me the valuable lessons of life and showing me how to live by conservative values.
- Chante Hopkins

"...every generation needs regeneration in order to move forward ... you are that new generation, expected to lead the charge for the next 25 or 50 years or for as long as it takes. Do not stray from the responsibility of eliminating from our midst any and all racial, social, economic, or political restraints that now exist in this great nation."

- Remarks given to the Howard University School of Law Class of 2006 by Professor Julian R. Dugas, Member, Howard University School of Law Class of 1949 & Lifelong Republican (1918-2014)

Authors' Note:

Is it Democrat Party or Democratic Party?

For the sake of parallelism, it's the Democrat Party. A Republican
is a member of the Republican Party, a Libertarian, a member of
the Libertarian Party, so on and so forth. Though the Democratic
Party makes it convenient to imply it is democratic, from what you
will find from this book, virtually nothing is *democratic* about the
Democrat Party. Therefore, we will refer to it as such.

By all means, feel free to do the same.

PREFACE

"We are in a weird place right now. It's hard to understand the context and culture of a political crisis when you are in the center of it, but here we are nonetheless." - NY Daily News

If you had told me this time last year that I would be a Republican, I would not have believed you. This book is about how I got from there to here, amidst this crazy election year no less.

There I was, at yet another crossroads in my life. I had gone through an intense election cycle in 2014 totally entrenched in the Democrat Party both from my own attempt at running for state delegate and then as a field organizer for the governor's race. Senator Barbara Mikulski had announced that she was retiring by that next January, and no surprise to anyone, my congressman, Chris Van Hollen, decided to run for the seat. "Open Seat" elections are rare especially in my region. When folks win a seat, they tend to stay in it for a long, long time. Voters just vote for the incumbent, barring any major scandal, and it seems like the bar for "kick the bastard out" is pretty high these days. So, last summer, I decided to run for Congress. I figured why the heck not. As the young ones say, #YOLO (You Only Live Once). For all I know, the next time could be a decade or two from now, and there's no telling what could happen to me or to the country. But seriously, I decided to run for U.S. Representative of Maryland's 8th Congressional District because I believed, we were at a critical moment in our state's and country's trajectory. Our district was in dire need of a representative willing to represent the people first and not just tow the party line or force an extreme agenda. Being a part of the first generation that may not do as well as their parents, I felt an immense personal responsibility to make sure that "all boats are prepared for the long haul." However, you came to this country and whether you go to college or not, I believe that we each must find a way to find purpose and move forward. We were so focused on finding a new approach to governing and we wanted our campaign to represent future-focused leadership. Once I began my Congressional race, Unaffiliated, I realized how both parties were focusing on particularly divisive issues. It frustrated me to know that we have not done anything to ensure economic sustainability, and we're at a critical moment where if we do not invest in our social and physical infrastructure now, we will fall behind.

Deciding to run for Congress set me on this unbelievable path that led me to the Republican Party. This year has been taxing, mind-blowing, heartbreaking, yet enlightening, and because of it I needed to write this story down so that even I can believe it. The only thing that I do know for sure is that this journey was God-led.

My name is Liz Matory, and…I'm a Republican.

You're probably thinking, *what's the big deal. Who cares, right?*

But for some reason, it's like a big deal for me to be a Republican. First, I haven't been one for long. I joined at the end of January 2016 to participate in our state's closed primary. Yes. I became an R during an election year. With all the craziness of Election 2016, I somehow found myself in the Republican Party.

Second, I'm a millennial, so it's virtually impossible for me to be a republican, right? (Well, I'm two years older than millennials. As a 1980 baby, I'm too young and not cool enough to be considered GenX. Our Gen, as I like to claim it, tends to not join groups let alone political parties. We say that we don't like to be labeled (yet we have become very good at articulating all the myriad of ways we identify).

Thirdly, and you'll read more about it later, when folks look at me, they automatically assume I'm a Democrat. To conservatives, I'm an American, but to others, I'm a Black *cis* woman, and therefore, by default, I cannot possibly be a Republican.

Let's face it. Everybody assumes that Black women will vote for the Democrat Party, without question. By being the most loyal voter base (voting all the time for the same party), a black woman's vote has become the least respected vote in the American electorate because it has become obscenely predictable. Since the one party can "count on" the support of a whole block of voters, it takes full advantage of that assumption, and in turn, takes the individual voter, the individual American, for granted. Now, the Republican Party hasn't had the greatest track record for wooing new supporters as of late (well, technically, wooing back old supporters). So, the prejudgment about me, and

American Citizens who look like me, remains.

Oddly, as "progressive" as our society has become, it feels more restraining. Being an American in the 21st Century, I must now explain what type of woman I am. It goes without saying that I'm a proud American. I am proud to be Black & first-generation (more on my heritage later). And I am proud to be a woman, but instead of just being a woman, I now must delineate that I was born female, identify as female, and have no intention of changing my identity or gender – that's what *cis* means FYI. These days there are women who weren't born women and are now women, so now us natural-born women must explain ourselves once again. I feel for transgendered folks. I do. Some of my closest friends are proud members of the trans community. But what do we do about menstruation? Cramps? Walking with our heads held high as women? We were just beginning to find our voices. I know. I know. That's a lot to take in all at once, but welcome to my world.

This is my point, with all this social shifting going on, I'm that much more astounded by the fact that it is MY new identification that seems so questionable. Much, much more on that later.

All I know is that I did _not_ plan on this.

I did not plan on leaving the Democrat Party, going indie, or becoming a Republican. Heck, I didn't even plan on running for Congress, at least not this soon.

I mean, as a D.C. native, you dream about Congress. Or, at least I did growing up. But as a D.C. resident, I couldn't be an official voting member of Congress. For those who are not familiar with civics or may have forgotten a bit, D.C. is not a state, and therefore, does not have traditional representation in Congress. It has a delegate (we call a congresswoman out of kindness), but that elected position does not afford the District a vote on the floor in the U.S. Congress. This setup relegates D.C.'s delegate to being the most powerful lobbyist in Congress. Washington D.C. has no governor...state legislature...or...county government (not a state, remember?). None of that. This leaves D.C.'s mayor as the most powerful mayor in the country, and its council the most powerful municipal legislative body. But, a congressman in Idaho has more power over D.C. than every single elected official in D.C. making Idahoans more influential on D.C. law than Washingtonians. Technically, every U.S. Representative from every state in the union controls D.C. residents allowing every U.S. citizen that lives outside of D.C. to have overarching say over District residents. Technically, Puerto Rico is more powerful than the District of Columbia with them being both a territory *and* a country.

But I digress.

If anything, growing up in Washington made The Hill an *im*possibility. Studying federalism in law school only made my exasperation worse. When I was accepted into the University of Maryland for business school, I asked my mentor, Former Baltimore Mayor Kurt Schmoke, for words of wisdom just in case one day I decide to run for anything. In his classic no nonsense way, he said simply, "consider your options."

Becoming a Marylander was almost as difficult as changing party affiliation. Being a D.C. Native, you pride yourself for being one of the rare birds that are born to the city. I do feel like I abandoned D.C., but I just couldn't afford to live there anymore. Like my residency to see your identity change from D to I to R, just to mark off something different, I did not realize how much something like this would change my identity. It changed how I defined myself different than how I had my entire life up until that point. Just like I had to relinquish the residency of my past to step into a conceivable future, I had to step away from that former attitude in order to become a *born again republican*.

> \- *L.M.*
> Silver Spring, MD
> November 2016

1 BEFORE ME

"People will not look forward to prosperity, who never look backward to their ancestors."
– Edmund Burke

Before we dive into the intricacies of Liz, and what my life is about, it is important that we first start with my family and the values that helped shape my ideology. The 1980s was a period of increased racial harmony and improved conditions for African Americans, but the divide between the haves and the have nots was beginning to grow. My upbringing was not typical though by this time in our progression it ought to be by now. My father and mother were both physicians (well, surgeons) at Howard University Hospital. They met at the Old Freedmen's Hospital. A bit of historical recap, after the Civil War, the federal government created an agency called The Bureau of Refugees, Freedmen, and Abandoned Lands (The Freedmen's Bureau) to reconstruct the war-ravaged country and support the newly freed slaves in the South. The Bureau assisted in the reunification of the families and the formal education of the newly freed people, and soon, fellow citizens. Many institutions were founded at that time, most notably was Howard University, named after the commissioner of the Freedmen's Bureau, General Oliver Otis Howard. By the way, this post-war, Reconstruction period, was heavily pushed by Radical Republicans who sought to fully integrate Blacks into American society and establish political footing. The plantation owners/the secessionist/Confederates/Southern Democrats fought violently against the assimilation and empowerment of Blacks. The most ferocious display was, of course, the Ku Klux Klan, which was formed to terrorize Blacks and White Republicans. I mention this brief history to provide context. The children of Howard University grow up knowing this history, but the party affiliation is somehow expunged from the memory. I believe to our collective detriment.

So back to Dad and Mom.

My father's name was William Earle Matory, Sr. (Mom would have me insert M.D., F.A.C.S. (which means that he was a fellow of the American College of Surgeons). He was born on October 1, 1928 in East St. Louis, Illinois to Willie Mae and James Matory. They were both a part of what was called the Great Migration when, at the turn of last century, Blacks from southern states like Mississippi fled the South to the North for better economic opportunities. This is how my kin came up to East St. Louis in 1913 when my grandfather was 24 years old. My grandmother followed him later when he gained his footing. The main industries were tanning, meatpacking, metalwork, and the railroad. James was a laborer for Swift & Co., a major meat packing plant headquartered in Chicago. Meat products and leather were transported via train across the country. As such, E. St. Louis was also an industrial and polluted area to live in, but people could make a living. It was known as the "Black part of town." When the migrants traveled north along the

8

Mississippi, they brought their creole traditions like the funeral Second Line with them. St. Louis, Missouri was where Whites lived, and the Blacks lived across the Mississippi River in E. St. Louis, Illinois. But back then, there was an economy. E. St. Louis is perhaps best known for being the birthplace of jazz legend Miles Davis, a childhood friend of my uncle and my father.

By 1917, thousands of Blacks were coming to E. St. Louis, and there was resistance to the population shift. Most notably when Black workers were brought in to replace white workers who went out on strike at a local Aluminum plant. On July 2nd, mobs of Whites entered black neighborhoods burning homes, lynching residents, and shooting people at random. Before burning houses, some rioters would board up doors and windows so inhabitants could not escape. Police refused to break up the riots. Between 40 to 250 people were estimated to have died. Ida B. Wells-Barnett was the first to report on the riots in her New Negro Fellowship Herald Press article, "The East St. Louis Massacre: The Greatest Outrage of the Century." Here is an excerpt from her writings:

> *Such is the history in part of one of the most dastardly crimes ever committed in the name of civilizations, on defenseless black men, women and children. That the State of Lincoln, Logan, Grant – three names made famous by their fight to give liberty to the black man – should furnish this black page for history, is the shame of all true American citizens. The world is at war because the race prejudice of one nation tries to dominate the other nations. The race prejudice of the United States asks Americans of black skins to keep an*

inferior place and when these Negroes ask an equal opportunity for life, liberty, and the pursuit of happiness, they are lynched, burned alive, disfranchised and massacred! Whenever a black man turns in this land of the free and home of the brave, - in industry, in civic endeavor, in political councils in the ranks of Christians (?) – this hydra headed monster confronts him; dominates, oppresses and murders him!

— Ida B. Wells-Barnett

Her report was held by United States Military Intelligence Division on Negro Subversives until it was released by the National Archives in 1986. The congressional hearing report on the riots was secreted by the Government because it believed the information would discredit the United States on the world stage during the first World War. My grandfather and his brother were drafted into the army on June 5, 1917 to fight in said war. A month before the riot broke out. Four Mississippi relatives were drafted into the war by September 12, 1918.

The East St. Louis Massacre/Riots are considered one of the worst race riots of the 20th Century and serve as a classic example of the aristocratic practice of pitting working class Americans against each other to cultivate enduring racial tension between Whites and Blacks. Apart from skin color, similarly situated people who have a common interest if unified would threaten The Elite's claim to power. Blacks were not allowed to join unions at the time. So, when union members walked out on their jobs, Blacks were available to fill them and continue production. The Democrat Party was also concerned that the influx of Blacks, who were Republicans, would negatively impact its political power in the region. Marcus Garvey's speech on the Massacre was made into a pamphlet and distributed throughout New York City and Harlem, which inspired the NAACP and other organizers to march in silence down 5th Avenue. Ten thousand Blacks participated. The relatively nascent, James Weldon Johnson led-NAACP requested an audience with the White House, but was refused. The president at that time was democrat Woodrow Wilson. The same president who showed the first motion picture to be viewed in the White House, D.W. Griffith's Birth of A Nation, the one about the founding of the Ku Klux Klan. That president did nothing.

When my father was growing up, there were three business families in E. St. Louis. Miles Davis's father was a dentist. The Millers ran, and still run, the mortuary. And our family, we were shoe cobblers. My grandfather owned and operated Matory's Shoe Repairing on 1501 Tudor Avenue. The family home was attached to the shop. My grandmother died while giving birth to the youngest brother, John Lee, when my father was two years old. The two young boys were sent to live with their Aunt Ida in Jackson, Mississippi. From age two to ten, Dad lived in Jackson. Back then there was farmland. His chores when he got old enough were bringing corn to the mill and tending to the family cow. His brother fell off a wall at school and Aunt Ida nursed him back to health at home because there was no place that would care for a black child. Though my great aunt tried her best, my father said his brother was never the same after that. This experience motivated him to pursue quality healthcare for all. When they were old enough, the two boys were sent back to East St. Louis to live with their father and sisters. Because their mother was no longer there, his eldest sister, Helen, raised the five other children. Dad was very close to Aunt Helen. He said he felt so indebted to her since she had so much responsibility placed on her before she had even hit puberty. I can remember when she passed away. That was the first (but not the last) time I saw my father's heart weep.

From what I know about Dad's upbringing, it was rather American. He, of course, went to Lincoln High School (there is a Lincoln High School in virtually every Black neighborhood just like there would eventually be a MLK or Barack Obama school in the subsequent years). And he said that he sang, *Danny Boy*, at the beginning of lunch or assembly or something like that. I always thought that was somewhat peculiar given the song was made popular with Irish-Americans, but it goes to show you how much our various cultures influence each other in this country. Dad graduated high school early actually. He said it was because he skipped two grades coming up from Mississippi. He said they hadn't taught handwriting when he left Mississippi and had already taught it by the time he returned to Illinois. Dad couldn't write legibly to save his life, but I think that's like a thing for physicians I've been told. He was 16 when he left home for Howard University in 1945. Howard at that time was the premiere institute of higher learning for African-Americans. Dad spoke about how excited he was to make the football team, only to lose his position the next year when the GIs came back from serving in the war. Our country and the capital were still extremely segregated. Dad said that they had to take the trolley all the way down to a bookstore near George Washington University to buy books. They were not allowed to shop downtown, and U Street was the only place they could socialize. My father would not recognize the area around Howard now. Though I'm sure he would be pleased to see the landmark theaters, Lincoln and Howard, restored.

Dad was super humble. He would lament about how he almost missed out on his dream of becoming a doctor because he failed Chemistry (mind you, I think I remember him saying he got a C!). But, he made his way. Graduated *cum laude*, served as president of his class, and attend Howard University College of Medicine. When I got a little older and did the math, I realized that Dad had my oldest brother, Earle (his junior) at age 22 when he had started medical school. When I asked him about it, when I was old enough to have the courage to ask, I asked him what happened. He said it was his duty to marry his first wife, Deborah, even though his father said he did not have to. Against his father's advice, Dad married because he said it was the right thing to do. Even until the end, through the bitter separation & divorce and when he married my mom, Dad never spoke negatively about Deborah. I never met her, oddly. Dad would just say; she is the mother of my children.

Dad and Deborah had two more children, my sister, Yvedt, and my brother, Randy. Yvedt was born in Japan when Dad was stationed there after the Korean War as a captain in the Air Force Medical Corps. This, I think, is one of the more peculiar aspects of my upbringing that I'm a part of two generations since my father was 80 when he passed in 2009. My older siblings grew up in the 50s and 60s and are contemporaries of my friends' parents, so my perspective is a bit warped. It was my siblings that dealt with desegregation. The oldest, Earle, was a member of the first class to integrate Coolidge High School. He went on to be one of the first Black players on the Yale football team. My sister attended Sidwell Friends; again, she was one of the first. And, Randy attended Maret, another D.C. prep school. So, when we younger two came along in the family, it felt like there was nothing groundbreaking to be done. Earle was already a plastic surgeon by the time I came of age.

13

My sister was constantly doing fellowships and kicking ass in the surgical oncology space throughout my lifetime. She even attended Columbia Business School while pregnant with her twins at the same time I was there for undergrad. And Randy, (his name is actually James Lorand Matory), got his PhD when I was 11, conducted his field studies in Nigeria and Brazil through my teen years, and is now at his second tenured professorship at Duke, his first was at Harvard. If I said we aren't a competitive family, I would be lying, but I don't think it was my parents' intention. If anything, it is just the nature of blended families. The burden of being a full generation younger than one's siblings. It's not like my father planned to create this environment for his children. I do believe that he loved his children deeply, and he created the most encouraging environment considering the circumstances. He never wanted the divorce to devastate his children; he did want to have more children and get a fresh start.

See, my father was an extremely accomplished man. He set the bar high for what I see men, fathers, husbands to be. After serving in Japan, he returned to Howard University Hospital (again, it was called Freedmen's Hospital back then) to practice surgery and stayed there until he retired. Though my father was a successful general surgeon, he was an innovator when it came to healthcare and medical education. He established the emergency medical program and introduced dialysis to the program at Howard. Dad started the first Family Practice program there incorporating different specialist provide outpatient services to post-op patients like cardiology, internal medicine, pediatrics, and obstetrics and gynecology (my mother was the OB-Gyn Dad hired for the first team). Dad also was the longest serving Continuing Medical Education Director for both the College of Medicine and the National

Medical Association. The NMA was established because the American Medical Association did not accept Blacks in its membership until 1968. The mission of the NMA is still to ensure that health care providers continue to receive the best education to provide the best standard of care for our diverse population. Medical education and access to quality medical care were Dad's passion. He was always in search of the latest techniques. His last trip before he died was up to Canada to visit their surgical simulation labs. A far cry from operating on dogs in the 70s. Dad even taught us how to suture on pigs feet. Dad was amazing, but I do know that my brother, Bill, and I benefited from coming later in his life. He was much more established and though he probably made it to less than 10 games over the course of our athletic careers, we know he was more available to us than perhaps the older children. I don't know how it was for them growing up, but I can remember Dad talking about how he always wanted to do right by all his children. He made a huge effort to have a distinct and fully loving relationship with each of his children. He tried not to "contaminate" one relationship with another. All I know is that my dad was the type of person who loved fully, his family, his colleagues, his work. At his funeral, I realized how completely my father loved. I think he singlehandedly ruined my concept of how people can be. As one of his classmates, Dr. Bezell said, he was touched by God.

My mom is awesome, and of course, I'm biased, but I have gotten to know my mom a lot more after my dad passed. When Dad was alive they were a couple and I dealt with them as a unit almost. Oddly, I should not admit that I had a more individualized relationship with my father, but when he died I got to see my mom more fully. Mom is Rita Rigor-Matory, M.D., F.A.C.S. Born in Manila, Philippines, and she

15

probably wouldn't want me to say what year. Though by saying that she was a war baby sort of gives her age away. One of Mom's first recollections was of her sitting on top my grandfather's shoulders yelling *Victory Joe! Victory Joe!* to the American soldiers who threw candy from their tanks as they rolled through the streets of Manila. That moment was two years after my grandmother had to escape the city for the countryside with her three young daughters. All electricity had been cut off and they had to leave in pure darkness. Fortunately, my grandmother (Lola) and her three girls made it safely to my paternal great grandfather's rice farm in Tarlac. Lola had sewn her valuables and documents into a pillow that she laid underneath my mother's head. During the war, Lolo (Tagalog for grandfather) had been captured by the Japanese and forced to march with other soldiers on the Bataan Death March. I was told that he managed to slip through his captor's bars because he was so emaciated. To get to victory, Lola had to nurse her husband back to health, malaria and all.

The stories of my mother's childhood and the type of womanhood that it forged affected me greatly. Everything from Lola being an entrepreneur and a pharmacist to how much of a full-on nerd my mom said she was. Lola finished her degree in pharmacy at age 19. After the war, she was a seamstress to not only provide income for the family of 9 (seven children they ended up rearing), but also to clothe said children. Lolo went back to school to get an engineering degree, and became a civil engineer gaining credit for the rebuilding of Manila, and modernizing the provinces after the war. According to my mom, she was a "bookworm," and also graduated high school early. She attended Universidad de Santo Tomas (UST), the oldest university in The Philippines and in Asia. Founded in 1611 by the Dominicans, UST exemplifies the complexity of the Filipino history. The Spanish ruled the Philippines for 356 years. Before they arrived, however, Muslims settled the southern islands. Catholicism has maintained a stronghold over most of the country. After the Spanish-American War, Spain lost the Philippines to the United States. Despite the colonizing forces, there are more than 100 languages spoken on the Philippine Islands with Tagalog being the predominate one. This dynamic causes many, particularly the educated Filipinos to be multi-lingual, speaking a native language like Tagalog, English and Spanish especially among the older generations. In 1992, The United States was asked to leave its naval post at Subic Bay and Clark Airbase, but in 2014, President Obama signed an agreement with the Philippines to allow for military presence in particularly to monitor China's encroachment into the South China Sea. I remember going to Manila for the first time to celebrate Lola and Lolo's 50th wedding anniversary when I was 7 years old. The reception was at Clark Air Base. I went back three more times, and was the only grandchild to go back as an adult. Even as late as 2002, I remember going to get my Lola's pension from the government. We had to take a picture of Lola with that day's newspaper to prove that she was indeed still alive. She was 93 when she passed away. I was glad I got to see her before she died. Though she was bedridden and had a few several cries of wanting to go, she was lucid until the end.

My mom arrived in the United States in 1966 after she graduated from UST. She started her postgraduate work in Massachusetts, and by the next year she moved to Washington to perform her residency at George Washington University. After doing an extra year for urology, Mom went down to Mississippi to work for the University of Mississippi in 1971. She stayed there for "one cotton picking season." She worked for the Community Health Improvement Project and had assignments in Mound Bayou and Vicksburg. When she arrived, she could not find an apartment that would rent to her. She ended up staying in Nurse's Dormitory at the hospital for a couple of months. The Department of OB-Gyn found a place for her eventually. Mom got another dose of Jim Crow while working at the maternity ward of the Vicksburg Hospital. When she made her first morning rounds of the labor room with the thirty-two midwives she was training, she witnessed all the expecting mothers lying down on the floor and not in the beds. Every bed was empty. When she asked someone about it, they whispered that the beds were reserved for the white patients. Immediately, my mom ordered that every pregnant woman be placed on beds. Afterwards, Mom was paged into the hospital director's office and was reprimanded. The director also warned her about which dining room she was allowed to use. To this Mom replied, "I'll eat wherever I want to eat." He called her an activist. Mom said she had no idea what and an "activist" was at the time; she just wanted to care for her patients.

I know these experiences allowed my parents to connect even more. Even though Mom came from the other side of the globe, she understood some of what my father had to go through his entire life. Dad never spoke about racism per se. He told me what his father said about blackness was, "Be proud of how dark your skin is because whatever you end up achieving in your life, folks will know a Black man did it." I will never forget watching Election Night 2008 with my father. All he kept on repeating was, "I can't believe it. I can't believe it." From his bed in the MICU at Howard University Hospital, Dad watched Barack Obama take the oath of office and George W. Bush taking his last flight over Washington in Marine One right before he died the week later. It was in that moment that I knew life would never be the same.

The main reason why I'm telling you all this backstory is because in the Democrat world, I was made to feel like my upbringing was somehow wrong or strange. I represented the achievement of a professional class, two-parent home with reliable income, not quite the economic deprivation narrative that Democrats enjoy exploiting. I was told that because I did not experience the "started from the bottom now we're here" tale that I would not be relatable to voters. I quickly realized that what they meant was that I don't fit the mold of what they think a Black woman leader should be in their society. I have experienced firsthand how myopic the liberal view is when it comes to people of color. Much more on this later, but I believe that your ancestors and your heritage affect your perspective greatly. I am well aware that I would not be who I am and what I am without my foremothers and forefathers. I want to finally hold my head high and not have to hide who I am, as I was told to do when I was a democrat.

2 HAD BEGUN TO WONDER

"It is a miracle that curiosity survives formal education."
– Albert Einstein

The talk of Republicanism wasn't that prolific for me until recently. Some of my family members are Republicans. I think everyone has that outspoken uncle who seems to speak in an entirely different language than the rest of the family. But for the most part, I spent more than most of my time in Democrat environments. The unshakable opinion Black Republicans is that they are bizarre and unusually estranged. Democrat counterparts reject the notion of political choice. All too often we assume that Blacks in America are Democrats by default. That assumption denies agency to an entire group of citizens. Growing up in D.C., attending Sidwell and Columbia, I was entrenched in the liberal point of view. But, I did have this one professor at Howard Law who was a staunch member of the GOP, Professor Julian Dugas. Professor Dugas was the keynote speaker at the Pinning Ceremony for our class in 2003. There we were, roughly 143 super green 1Ls sitting, sweating, waiting to commence our law school gauntlet with absolutely zero clue as to what to expect. We just knew that we had voluntarily enlisted in the pending three years of torture. There, standing no more than 5' 7" in a classically pristine lawyer suit, almond skin, and wavy hair was Professor Dugas, our oldest, and longest serving professor at the law school. With his impeccable Georgian accent, Professor Dugas instructed us on *what it means to be a Howard Law Student.*" Off the bat, Dugas spoke about the task before us as we began our journeys at "the birthplace of the 20th century's Civil Rights Movement, where in the past, giants in law gathered as one, to plan a better America." We were to be law students that were to not only be as scholars of the law, but also be "brave and courageous enough to confront and fight any and all forms of injustice." He defined us as "our future visionaries, expected to devise new ways and means to remind the nation of its responsibility to fulfill the promises of the Constitution, not by words, but by deeds." At the time, all of this sounded super overwhelming, but he had such genuine faith in us young Howard Law students, that even though we didn't know how we would make our mark, we understood that there was plenty of hard work still to be done. You may be wondering why I'm making such a huge deal about Howard Law. It is because my law school was the institution that compelled our modern society through segregation and as of that day, Professor Dugas and the rest of the faculty compelled us to build on that legacy. I took it to mean by any means necessary.

Professor Dugas was one of my all-time favorite professors. Shortly after his speech, I found out that he pledged by father to the fraternity of Kappa Alpha Psi in 1945/6 at Howard. So, from that day, he kept his eye on me. When conversations around the 2004 Election took over the campus, I recall asking Professor Dugas who he was supporting, and he said President Bush of course because he was a lifelong Republican. Lifelong Republican? I had no idea. I think I even said that out loud to him, but I thought that all Black people were democrats! He sagely stated, "The Republican Party freed the slaves; therefore, I will always be a Republican." It was that simple. Those conversations with Professor Dugas were some of the most intellectually jarring conversations I had in law school. Before I met him, I never thought about Black People being Republicans. It was not for my lack of education. I went to some of the best schools in the country, but I never until that time was exposed to the notion.

Even after taking history courses from seminal professors like Eric Foner and Thaddeus Russell at Columbia, the history lessons seemed to always leave the power of Republicanism out. If they mentioned it, it surely didn't register. No other conversation left me with more questions than the conversations with Professor Dugas (and believe me at Howard Law, we had some doozies). He was the youngest member of the legal team that brought *Bolling v. Sharpe*. It was the companion Supreme Court case for *Brown v. Board of Education* that desegregated schools in the District. Since D.C. was and is not a state, other cases are brought to change laws that will affect the municipality. Yes, that did make him a contemporary of our most famous alumnus, U.S. Supreme Court Justice Thurgood Marshall. Professor Dugas pretty much forged what is the D.C. Government from the time that it gained Home Rule in the 1970s. So, when he spoke, he had real authority in my and a great many other's opinion. These conversations, borderline debates, with him about his Republicanism left me truly confused. His statement, party affiliation, and belief was diametrically opposed to everything I had been taught and thought my entire life. Simply put, I thought that the Republican Party was just a bunch of old white guys who didn't like Black people or poor people, and only loved money and war. If that were true, how could someone like our Professor Dugas be a part of something like that? Turns out there is a perfectly logical reason why someone like Julian Dugas was a lifelong Republican. It took me a few more years (try, a full decade) to figure it out, but it gives me much relief to know that he was not wrong. With the knowledge that I have garnered now, I appreciate his words more now than ever before. He is one of the reason why I have been able to survive the bumps and the bruises of becoming a **Born Again Republican**:

> You are [at Howard University School of Law] to train
> to become leaders of tomorrow, not followers, creators
> of cutting-edge initiatives designed to overcome the
> myriad problems faced daily by African-Americans
> especially, and others similarly situated, as they struggle
> to enjoy the full rights of citizenship.
>
> - Professor Julian R. Dugas

The next time I thought about Republicanism was during the Special Election campaign of my dear friend, Marion Christopher Barry. By January 2015, I had already lost my attempt to serve in the Maryland House of Delegates, and as a former member of the Maryland Democratic Party field team, I was still numb by the stupefying defeat in the 2014 Governor's Race. By then, both A.J. Cooper, our friend and local luminary, and Christopher's father, Marion, had died back-to-back. Christopher reached out to me to help him run and to complete his father's term on the D.C. City Council. We had not seen each other since our first year of college. Admittedly, like many of the folks who grew up with Christopher, I had only heard about him from time to time via his periodic goings-ons caught by the various news outlets. Though

Life had brought us on divergent paths, time relativity kicked in when we reconnected. After all, we had known each other since we were toddlers.

Prior to my time with Christopher, I had spent a year "East of the River" a few years back when I helped found Excel Academy, the first all-girls public charter school in Washington. Sadly, most D.C. residents stick to their sides of town. Before then, I was naive to what mass unemployment or multiple minimum wage jobs to make ends meet looked like. Very few of my friends gave birth before they were 20, though a few by then had at least one abortion. I was unaware that since the time I graduated high school, Ward 8 had not had a single major grocery store until it received one in 2007 (there is still only one grocery store for 70,000 residents). Just like other charter schools, we believed that we could change the trajectory of families and communities by placing our laser focus on children, and in the case of Excel Academy, on girls as early as three years of age. We believed wholeheartedly that education was the great equalizer. But, the moment I joined Christopher on his campaign that January, I realized that the scale of inequity had become so severe that schoolhouse efforts would remain inadequate if something wasn't done immediately about the conditions and consequences of life on the Southside. Even as a D.C. native, Ward 8 felt like a world away even though it was physically only a handful of miles away.

In many ways, the District of Columbia is still a segregated city. Like the rest of America, D.C. still has distinct divisions based on race, class, economies, and economics despite decades old integration efforts. Growing up, Rock Creek Park was the de facto dividing line where Whites lived 'West of the Park' and Blacks lived East of it, but since

2000, the city has changed dramatically. Fifty more census data tracts became gentrified with home values increasing in some areas by 236%. D.C. at its peak had a population around 800,000 in the 1950s. Blacks had steadily left the South for Northern cities to flee Jim Crow racism and to find opportunities for employment. Whites began to flee cities particularly when desegregation was mandated. Over 300,000 white residents left for the suburbs, like Montgomery and Prince George's County, making D.C. a majority black city by the end of the 1950s. Note that many neighborhoods like Wheaton, Silver Spring, Kensington, and Chevy Chase actively restricted homeownership based on race through restrictive covenants (prohibited by 1967) and carried out real estate discrimination clean through the 1970s. Even the current 96% white make up of Chevy Chase remains suspect given the demographics of the rest of Montgomery County and the rest of the Washington Metropolitan Area. (I, personally, live on the MD/DC border between Chevy Chase and Silver Spring, and grew up 2.4 miles away in D.C.'s Ward 4.) Before desegregation, Black lawyers, professors, doctors, teachers, mechanics, and custodians all lived in the same neighborhoods because Whites prohibited other races from living amongst them. But when riots broke out in 1968 after the assassination of Dr. Martin Luther King, Jr., many middle class black families fled the cities to the suburbs as well. Those who remained in the city moved uptown to the Northeast and Northwest quadrants of the city. Though there are some portions in the city that are racially and economically diverse, the city and its suburbs are both racially and economically isolated to this day. Central city and ex-urban enclaves changed even more with mass immigration of folks from Central and South America beginning in the 1980s through the 1990s and rapidly from the turn of the 21st Century.

Every day I would drive down from Montgomery County to Southeast D.C. for the campaign. Driving through every gentrified neighborhood to get there, I would think to myself:

How can things be so different for people, this late in the game?

How can we call this progress if we are still so segregated?

Even access to food is ridiculous. With six Whole Foods that service the Northwest quadrant and just one supermarket in Ward 8 for its 70,000 residents, how can anyone consider that any of this is okay? Many a night Christopher and I would debate and discuss these realities. Ward 8 was like a war zone with most of the men between the ages of 16 and 45 either dead, in or just out of jail. Legally mandated separation of fathers from children leaves mothers or grandmothers alone to care for their children. Grown men (and women) try to find decent work, but to no avail. The schools, if they were doing all they can, cannot compete with the deleterious norm of truancy, drug use, and low personal and societal expectation. Christopher and I both came to the conclusion that more government would not permanently resolve any of these tribulations. We both believed that there had to be a better way, a more sustainable way to fix this. After all, it's not rocket science. To my disbelief, Christopher admitted to me that if he could be a Republican, he would. Back then, I thought he had to be kidding.

3 LIFE AS A LIBERAL

"If you're not a liberal at twenty you have no heart, if you're not a conservative at forty you have no brain." – Winston Churchill

Growing up in Washington, I didn't have much of a choice in my party affiliation. D.C. has been a Democrat stronghold ever since it gained Home Rule in the 1970s. I only remember one Republican elected official, Councilwoman Carol Schwartz. As it stands to this day, D.C. is still a one-party town. Of course, the bi-partisan seat of the Nation's government exists within the borders of Washington, but every D.C. resident knows, there are two Washingtons. Politics is the industry in Washington. Presidential elections and inaugurations are our Olympics. Notable politicians and reporters were our celebrities, and just like Los Angeles, their kids were our classmates, as was the case for me. These kids were friends, teammates, and classmates, and are only mentioned to give you context for the seemingly random, uber-liberal, alternate universe I grew up in. By no means are these bragging rights, if anything, going to school at a place like Sidwell in a city like D.C., made me even more of a skeptic when it came to politics and the world that the media creates. Ever since I was two (with Chris at Tots Developmental

Center), there was palpability to this kind of affiliation and connection. A moment on Tots – Carlise Davenport began Tots in 1962. For the next 48 years, Tots was the seminal school for the children of professional Blacks in Washington. There, we celebrated Black Excellence unapologetically. We studied George Washington Carver, Frederick Douglass, Booker T. Washington, Shirley Chisolm, and Walter Fauntroy all before we turned nine years old. History was history unabridged. The Barry Family gave us the most intimate comprehension of our leadership, its good and bad aspects. Since the school was extremely small and selective, we weren't just classmates, we were family. Every graduate knows that Tots remains the most challenging school we have ever attended. There, instructors did not allow you to get anything wrong. Ultimately, we would not have achieved what we all have without the nurturing and strong foundation Mrs. Davenport provided for her children.

I remember feeling this odd sense of duty thrust onto us at such a young age just by growing up in an environment sprinkled with children of prominence. There was an unwritten rule back then that we classmates were their protectors. Unlike other schools, we witnessed firsthand how different/difficult life seemed for them, and that their childhoods were never quite like the rest of ours. Adolescence is awkward enough and for some of the kids walking down the street was even an ordeal. Anything they did or said could be held against them harsher than any of the rest of us. Normalcy never truly existed, but we did our best to do our part. In turn, all our perspectives were like no one else's. Because elected officials and members of the media were the parents of my friends and classmates, perhaps I still expect more from public servants and members of the press. When I was younger, I didn't decipher a distinction from other professional parents besides living a life of exposure. But, I assumed they had to work that much harder to care for their children for them to survive that existence that had been thrust upon them. Unfortunately, Christopher did not survive the pressure in the end. His limelight became lethal.

Sidwell hid me from the "real world" in many ways, but I love Sidwell Friends. I will forever be grateful for the knowledge and relationships that developed my intellect and character, but it is the ultimate bubble. We had environmental science as a mandatory class in middle school. We studied Latin American History a year before we studied U.S. History. I think our school had one of the earliest Chinese language classes in the region, which was phenomenal. Diversity Club was routine and the Investment Club was a novelty. One of my white friends was even elected president of the Black Student Union. Our school community fully embraced sexuality and identification in my opinion, but I could be ignorant to the difficulties faced. Sidwell is a Quaker school and the easiest way I can describe the religion is that it is very egalitarian and kindness-driven. Teachers and coaches are for the most part called by their first names. And, we did not have GPAs, class rank, or valedictorians. All the above is valuable no doubt, but I knew even then that this environment was more of an alternate universe. I can only recall perhaps two conservative or Republican classmates over the course of my nine years there. I lived, breathed, and was indoctrinated into liberal thought since I was nine years old. I was oblivious to alternative thinking making my conversion even more severe.

I never questioned my democratic affiliation or liberal beliefs until I was 35 years old. And, yes. That was only a year ago. Even when

I ran for state delegate in 2013-14, the Republican Party was still just the other party. So, I never considered running as anything else other than a Democrat. Clear through my 2014 campaign for state delegate, I never thought of being anything other than a Democrat. Through college, law school, and even business school, I still only had two or three Republican friends. I didn't think much of it. Besides, everything I knew about Republicans was foreboding: *they were mean, un-inclusive, racist bigots who only wanted our country to fight wars and take away women's rights because they hated women (and gays and Blacks for that matter).* Mind you, I never once stopped to think that my belief of what Republicans were was singularly formulated by fellow liberals.

4 THE SUMMER I CLAIMED MY INDEPENDENCE

"Independents are rising. They are rising to the challenge of making American democracy."
— Jacqueline Salit, president of IndependentVoting.com

In May 2015, I returned my focus back to Maryland after working with Christopher in his Ward 8 race in D.C. I recalled that Senator Mikulski announced her retirement and that Congressman Van Hollen decided to run for the senate seat, but an open seat for the 8th congressional hadn't sunk in for me until that summer. I never thought of running for it until I attended the Annual Gala for the Maryland Democratic Party. Having toiled as a field organizer in the 2014 Gubernatorial Race and ran as a candidate myself, the Gala was like a family reunion. I got to know a lot of wonderful people over the few years, party staples, elected officials, staffers, etc. With such a brutal election year, being at the gala was heartening to reconnect. So it was not out of the ordinary for me to take a picture with Congresswoman Donna Edwards of the 4th Congressional District and post it to Facebook. And with one Facebook post, I gained clarity.

See, by the time of the Gala both Chris Van Hollen AND Donna Edwards decided to run for the Senate seat and already, it became a contentious race. I didn't realize how brutal it was until I posted a picture of me with the congresswoman and wrote the words:

> *"Congresswoman Donna Edwards!! Thank you for being an #inspiration #groundbreaker #womenlead"*

This post got me uninvited to volunteer for the Van Hollen campaign. I had signed up to volunteer in his Kensington field office for several reasons: 1) he was my congressman, my first congressman ever to be exact, and I wanted to support his efforts, 2) Kensington was a community that I had grown to love over the last year during my own campaign, and I missed being there so I wanted to get back around the way, and 3) I considered Van Hollen a true leader not only in the county, but because of how he had treated me as a younger challenger. Most elected officials shunned me as a challenger who chose to run again incumbents, but he truly saw my passion and will to serve. Though he never endorsed/supported me officially (regrettably), I know he understood me, and for that reason alone, I wanted to do what I could to support his efforts. But when I received an email from a senior staffer informing me that I was no longer wanted as a volunteer, I was astonished. I didn't understand where this was coming from after everything. But, it was my Facebook post. I had heard that political people get nervous about social media, pictures and the like especially during political races, but I didn't understand how what I posted would make me be an un-volunteer. So, I asked and the answer I received boils down to three things: *gossip, gender, and race*. Apparently, someone from the Montgomery County Dems whispered to the Van Hollen camp that I was going to work with Donna and that I was playing the Van Hollen camp. *What B.S.!* First, I had just finished a taxing campaign in Washington, and I wasn't ready to join officially on another one at that time. Second, I hadn't thought of working for Donna nor had her people asked me about it. Third, why didn't someone ask me personally!!! I mean it's not like they didn't have my contact information. And, someone could have easily asked me since I was right there at the same event. Instead, someone thought it would be helpful to spread an incorrect statement about me and yes that person wanted to cause harm. Sadly, I know exactly who it was, and I know that person has only malicious and self-serving intent. That person is the reason why I traveled an hour every day to work in Baltimore County for the Gubernatorial and not five minutes away in the local field office. The fact that it was someone from Montgomery County, the place that I call home, is what is so disheartening. There is supposed to be some sort of camaraderie and trust built up through participating with the local party, but in that moment, I realized that there is zilch.

The Chris Van Hollen v. Donna Edwards for Barbara Mikulski's seat epitomizes the problem that IS the Democrat Party. First, Barbara Mikulski is the longest serving woman in the U.S. Congress, and one of the first to win her seat without inheriting it from her husband or father. This one woman is a walking billboard for feminism all by herself. And so, when Chris Van Hollen stepped up to run for her seat, it created a democratic dilemma. Democrats hang their hats on identity politics. Whether it's race, gender, gender identity, or sexual orientation, labels are their everything. Putting Van Hollen's service and record a side, he was and is (and from what I know, will always be) a white guy. Could or should a white guy replace Barbara in the Senate? Should or shouldn't a woman replace THE ultimate woman senator? And when you add another "progressive" interest into the mix, why not promote the one Black woman who is also a congressperson or how about Congressman Elijah Cummings who is also Black and represents the City of Baltimore? In addition, both members of congress represent the largest areas of African-Americans in the state. Cummings, Edwards, and Van Hollen have virtually identical voting records and are as equally "progressive" as the next one. If race and gender are so important to the party, why didn't they make a bigger push to fight for diversity? If the Democrat Party were so interested in making history, why wouldn't they fight to make history here in Maryland?

It's because the Democrat Party doesn't care about Black people or Women.

I know that's a harsh statement, but think about it. If the Democrat Party truly cared about race or gender, there ought to have been a deliberate move to replace the one of only two senate seats of diversity with another person of diversity. I have already spoken about my admiration for Chris Van Hollen, but if diversity is that important to progressivism, even he would have stepped aside to promote the cause, but he didn't. The political operatives across the state knew that Van Hollen was "promised" the seat, and that Donna Edwards would get virtually no support from The Establishment since she wasn't part of the plan. It's like they collectively said, "How dare she think she can run for the Senate. We didn't give her permission." Her campaign was an insult to the establishment, and they will do whatever it takes to not see her succeed. Obviously, when the opportunity arouse, which it actually did, the Democrat Party chose not to take the opportunity make the play for progress.

If *they* thought about Donna Edwards that way, then I shouldn't have been surprised by how they thought of my running, without their permission. It is no wonder then that with my candidacy for State Delegate in 2014 that a bullying political operative and scheming elected officials all contrived to declare that I was, and I quote, "too educated and privileged to be the first Black woman elected to the State House from Montgomery County. Voters would not relate to me, so...." I will never forget how those words made me feel when I heard that (outside of a charity event no less). Why would voters have a problem with me being educated and for privileged? As one of the most affluent legislative districts in Maryland (and country even), how would Montgomery County voters not be able to relate to me? - since a fair number of primary voters either grew up like me or were raising their children in a similar fashion. Then, it hit me like a ton of bricks. It's because I'm not White that they "wouldn't relate." And, it's not about relating necessarily. It's the fact that the peanut gallery in their prejudgment presumed that liberal white voters could not support a rich black chick to represent them. They are used to seeing black women as single mothers just barely getting by – someone that they would support out of pity and say how hard her life must be. They assumed that voters could not accept me as an equal, or heaven forbid, more accomplished than they were. Simply put, promoting someone like me would not fit the limited image that the Democrat establishment maintained of us!

Before you go and blame the black chick, just take a moment and look throughout the 2016 congressional races in Maryland. The more

diverse candidates are actually Republican! The Democrat candidates for
the General Election are ALL men, and by that token if they succeed,
Maryland will have an all-male congressional delegation for the first
time in 39 years. I warned about this phenomenon last fall; and it is
partly the reason why I became an indie. The Democrat Party could have
considered gender (since they make such a HUGE deal about it) by
supporting Joseline Peña-Melnyk in the 4th Congressional, but if you
were wondering what happened to the Lt Governor who lost last year's
governor's race, that's where he finally landed. The Republican Party on
the other hand has two women and a Black man running for congress. I
witnessed their primaries, and the candidates did not play the gender or
race cards to survive their elections. They made the case to the voters
based on their merits. Amie Hoeber in the 6th Congressional is a career
foreign policy expert and military operative running in the second most
conservative district in the state. Kathy Szeliga is running against the
aforementioned Chris Van Hollen, and she made her case by telling
voters that when she and her husband first got married all they had was a
beat-up car and love. She worked odd jobs and waited tables and they
worked hard to become business owners. Corrogan Vaughn is making
perhaps the toughest case to run against Elijah Cummings in the 7th
Congressional, the area that includes the City of Baltimore and fragments
of two suburban counties. Because they are both Black men, Corrogan
can now make a more neutral case and contrast his conservative
principles to Cummings liberal governance. I believe that voters are
beginning to pay a lot more attention to their options. They crave
something different because they can no longer afford business as usual
any longer.

It is obvious that there is a shortage of next generation elected officials, electeds of diversity, and women in public office. 65% of officeholders are white men, allowing them to make up two-thirds of America's elected officials, though they only make up 31% of the U.S. population. That means a minority of the population is making major decision for 69% of us that they may not fully understand, and it makes you wonder if it matters that they care. It is hurtful to know that our government is not representative of its people, making it not only problematic but also ineffective. Let me take a minute to note how Black women's strength at the polls has not translated into political representation. Of the 102 female members of the 113th Congress, 15.7 percent (16) are African American. Of the 1,787 women who serve in a state legislature today, only 242 of them are black (13.5%). Part of me wishes I did not have to talk smack about my former party. I wish I didn't have to single out the party that consists of my former *compadres*. I still hold most them in regard, and appreciate them as human beings, friends and former colleagues. But, I just thought that the party that professed to champion diversity would readily champion candidates of diversity. But as soon as I saw the malarkey surrounding the Van Hollen v. Edwards race, I recognized the latent bigotry that existed in the Democrat Party. When push comes to shove, it is not fully invested in furthering diversity sincerely. It only deems progress permissible when it is on its terms. The deficiency of left-wing politics is that after fifty plus years of vigorously celebrating (more like exploiting) the moral supremacy of every cultural group, our political system remains, one of minority rule.

The next shift of my conscience occurred when I spent time surveying the 8th Congressional. I knew that Maryland did a brutal redistricting in 2010, but I never knew the extent of the destruction until I traversed my district. Prior to the 2010 gerrymandering, the 8th Congressional was made up of mostly Montgomery County, the area just north and west of the District of Columbia. Let me quickly explain gerrymandering. It is the job of our states to regulate legislative redistricting, while they may be subjected to several judicially imposed limitations, these are rarely ever understood by the general electorate. Often a region is redistricted without the knowledge of voters. Let's start at the point in the 1960s, the Supreme Court decided (including the *Reynolds v. Sims* case in Alabama) legislative districts cannot have great disparities in the number of people in them because disparities give voters in smaller-populated districts greater voting power in violation of the Fourteenth Amendment's Equal Protection Clause. This rule has required states to redistrict after each census to equalize the district populations that transition over each decade. This highly contrasts the drastic congressional redistricting, in which there may be no deviation from strict population equality, thus the Court has allowed state and local redistricting to deviate somewhat from strict equality for legitimate reasons, to reasons of commonality such as preserving city or county boundaries, or even worse the preservation of one's own political party. Such was the case was in 2010-2011, when the Democrats in the Maryland legislature took it upon themselves to redraw the voting districts in hopes of creating an all-Democrat congressional delegation.

The Supreme Court judicially allows redistricting to be the responsibility of the states, however, it is highly important to note that under Section 2 of the Voting Rights Act states must create districts in which racial minorities have the ability to elect candidates of their choice. These districts are known as "majority-minority districts" certain conditions, as long as there is compelling evidence that the minority group is sufficiently large and geographically compact, therefore possible to draw a majority-minority district, and proof of "racially polarized voting," meaning that Whites and voters of color tend to vote for different candidates. All of this can be done under the judicial limitations stipulated by The Supreme Court if states do not intentionally dilute the votes of some voters based on race under the Fourteenth and Fifteenth Amendment. Under Maryland's current system, the governor and legislature decide how electoral districts are drawn. The new commission would disallow any politician from participating. But let's be clear: the sophisticated manipulation of congressional districts in Maryland is a direct threat to our right to vote.

Gerrymandering can and has rigged our political system into polarizing partisan outcomes, never quite allowing the representative to fully reflect the voters.

All in all, the most destructive effects of gerrymandering and closed party primaries is the disenfranchisement of tens of millions of independent voters, according to a Gallup poll 47% of the U.S. electorate – now consisting of more people than that which exists in either major party.

Maryland was said to be the southern-most northern state and northern-most southern state in the Union, and in many ways, has inherited that legacy. Montgomery County, as mentioned before, had been the wealthiest of the counties in Maryland and the district encompassed similarly minded, for the most part liberal, residents. Prior to the 2012 election, there were six Democrats and two Republicans representing the state of Maryland in the US House. But the composition of the district changed immediately in the 2012 election when they stretched the 8th Congressional north from the D.C. border all the way up to the Pennsylvania border, and brought the 6th congressional south from Western Maryland through Montgomery County. With the election of John Delaney, Democrats got rid of Republican Congressman Roscoe Bartlett leaving Andy Harris as the one Republican to represent the congressional district that snakes down from the Pennsylvania border over to Maryland's Eastern Shore. The legislature also manipulated the congressional lines of both the 3rd and the 7th District to guarantee rock solid Democrat strongholds. But when it came to full out disenfranchisement of entire communities, nowhere in the state got it worse than in the 8th District. The moment that the Democrat-led legislature outstretched the 8th, rural and conservative votes were literally cancelled out by the denser populated liberal votes in the south. Of the 481,693 registered voters in Maryland's most populated congressional district only 52% are registered as Democrats, leaving the other 48% of voters registered as Republican, unaffiliated, Green, and Libertarian unrepresented in our "one party rule" state. Because Maryland Democrats have so skillfully manipulated the Congressional District maps to insure Democrat winners, the Democrat Party primary in Maryland is de facto and becomes the decisive election for the House. Sadly, the 48% of Marylanders not registered as Democrats get no vote, because of closed primaries, their votes in the general election typically does not matter because gerrymandering has predestined the outcome and deprived the voters of any real say in the November election.

As I considered running for the 8th, I immediately jumped at the opportunity to meet with Democrats in Frederick because I had become so accustomed to life in the D.C. and the immediate suburban area, I knew I needed to know more. One of the greatest advantages of Democrats over Republicans is their use of field organizing. Mind you, the Maryland Democratic Party is the oldest and longest established political party in the history of political parties, so it has a slight (meaning huge) advantage. As such there exists a Rural Democratic Summit every year here in Maryland. That year, the meeting was held in Frederick. Before that meeting, I had thought about running, but I wasn't sure until I met the members. From that meeting onward, I knew that there would be a fissure between the ideology of the Democrat candidates and the people they would seek to serve. It's no secret that once in office, Black women champion the interest of average citizens and underrepresented populations supporting progressive agendas surrounding education, healthcare, and economic sustainability. Historically, only 31 Black women from 13 states have served in U.S. Congress *EVER*, so of course I knew that running to be a U.S. Representative would be a huge undertaking, but with every person I met, I knew that I had to step up to the plate.

To this day, I don't know what got into me. All I remember is being there, watching, witnessing, and listening to the disconnect. There the supposed candidates were gliding through the crowd, shaking hands, grinning, but not paying much mind to the participants. If they did pay attention to what folks had to say, they would have heard members lament that they feel like the Democrat establishment there in Maryland had forgotten about them. They would have heard from the Rural Democrats that they are God-fearing, and that the establishment makes them feel wrong for believing and seeking to follow Jesus Christ. If they had concerns about abortion and ending life, they had to keep it to themselves for fear of being labeled a fundamentalist. I saw their frustration and felt the exact same way – invisible to those who should have cared.

But, immediately after I announced my intent to run, a state delegate came up to me and warned about how much money it would take to campaign for the seat. He said he thought about it, but since one of his friends was running, he wouldn't run against her besides it would cost too much (one Democrat candidate ended up wasting $12 Million of his own money to run and lose - can you imagine how many Americans could acquire a trade, eat decent food, learn to read, pay for a safe place to live with that kind of money?!?). The next morning yet another state delegate came up to me and said that people would have a hard time pronouncing my last name, Matory (pronounced maTory and that's funny, I still can't pronounce his). That *non*-congratulations were right before a former elected literally laughed in my face when I told her I was going to run for the seat. African-American women face distinct hurdles to political participation. We, women of non-anglo heritage, are less likely to be encouraged to run for office, and more likely to be discouraged from running compared to men and white women. Despite discouragement (or perhaps because of it), I knew that I had to run for this seat. At the end of the day, it wasn't even about me, but about the residents of District 8. There was so much more diversity lumped into it that I knew the Democrat Party would never fully appreciate. I had made up my mind. I did want to bust through race and gender stereotypes, but more importantly, I knew how it was to be cast aside. I would stand in the intersection between the metropolitan and a newly gained rural electorate. We would fight to represent the *ENTIRE* district, not just the liberal political and media elite. The advice Establishment Liberals did give included warnings about how racist places like Frederick County

44

were, KKK members, Confederate Flag, etc., don't door knock up there because you'll get shot, and the like. None of that had anything to do with the reality that I experienced. What I experienced firsthand was just people worried about their family's future. What would their children be able to do, if they were lucky enough to graduate from school? Where would they work and earn a decent living? How could they keep their family farm or their small business? How are they going to pay their own bills or take care of their aging parents? Because what's been going on is not helping. I thought that the only way our district could have equitable representation would be if I left the Democrat Party, and went independent. Again, I had no idea or intention of becoming a Republican.

The gerrymandering combined with the closed primary/democrat party stranglehold motivated me to become an independent. When speaking to democrats about our state's gerrymandering, I usually get the reply, "well, the GOP does it worse!" I refer to the old adage: two wrongs don't make a right. For democrats to gerrymander successfully, they must make the districts harsher because they have to dip into the various urban regions in order to tap into to concentrations of democrat votes by relying heavily on the votes of union members and Black folks. I would argue that Maryland is one of the harshest and most deleterious examples of gerrymandering ever conducted by the Democrat Party.

In the past year, the Supreme Court has ruled the gerrymandering of three states unconstitutional by violating the First and Fifteenth amendment. Because North Carolina and Maryland are two of the most gerrymandered states, Chante, my campaign manager and co-author of this book, fully understood my political frustrations with the systems disenfranchised voting practices. Chante is a registered voter in

North Carolina's 1st congressional district, a district so distorted it's referred to as an inkblot, intricately weaving through 24 of NC 100 counties. The length of the district's perimeter, according to the lawsuit, is 1,319 miles — "almost precisely the distance from Chapel Hill to Austin, Texas." A panel of federal judges ruled, this past March, that North Carolina lawmakers used racial gerrymandering to draw at least two of the state's thirteen congressional districts. "This ruling by all three judges is a vindication of our challenge to the General Assembly of North Carolina writing racially biased 'apartheid' voting districts to disenfranchise the power of the African-American vote," said the Rev. William Barber, president of North Carolina's NAACP chapter. This statement highlights the sentiments felt here in Maryland, we must work collectively in order to establish a nonpartisan system for drawing our state's voting maps. For decades, partisan gerrymandering has deprived voters of having a *REAL* choice and a voice in our elections. Fortunately for us, a growing number of citizens and leaders across the political spectrum agree that states should adopt an independent redistricting process. I pray that strong advocacy can save us from another decade of civic injustice.

As if gerrymandering isn't enough, the degradation of our representative government in Maryland is only exacerbated by its closed primary system. Elections have two parts, people. The general election AND the primary that comes months before. The average voter only goes out and votes during the November election with most folks usually saying, "Don't we vote in November?" But the dye is already cast by then, especially in a closed primary system. Slightly fewer voters participated in the 2016 primaries compared to the 2008 and 2012 election, the national turnout dropped one percentage point to 30 percent according to FairVote. Almost all states, including Maryland, saw higher participation in Republican primaries and lower participation in Democrat primaries. During the 2012 Primary election voter turnout was a whopping 17.5% in CD-8 and only 18.2% statewide! The Democrats trickled to the polls at 17% statewide while the Republicans showed their strength in numbers by turning out 28.6% of voters. This turnout helped elect Republican Governor Larry Hogan. Voters are more likely to participate in general elections because they acknowledge the importance of choosing a presidential candidate. Maryland proved that so by churning out 74% of voters in the 2012 General election. Again, Republicans used their political strength to show up Democrats at the polls, with 77% of their registered voters participating in the general election. Here in Maryland we have a closed primary, meaning that only party members can vote in their party's primary. Remember, political parties are membership organizations. They have virtually nothing to do with governing. They are literally just vessels of association. If you do not officially register with either the Democrat or Republican Party here in Maryland, you cannot choose the candidates that will survive onto the General. (For my Green Party comrades, yes you have an official party here as well, but as you well know, the major parties exclude your participation from the government-financed, sanctioned primary procedures. For reasons having nothing to do with democracy.) According to the omniscient Pew Research Center, more Americans now identify as Independent than either party, particularly Millennials. This reality causes most of the voting population to exist outside the selection process of our political leaders. In a place like Maryland, voters must register as either Democrat or Republican to have a voice in the election. What pushes Maryland's political scheme over the edge is the dominance of the Democrat Party, especially in a place like Montgomery County. The craziest thing about this progressive bastion of society is that there is, as of now, only one (1) republican elected official in the entire county of now one million residents. The town councilman of Kensington is a great guy, but there are more than just a handful of Republicans that live and pay taxes in Montgomery County. Many a conservative begrudgingly register as a Democrat to "have a voice" in government. In a place like Montgomery, and perhaps the rest of the state, voters are browbeaten to register as Democrats even when they do not share the views of the now hyper-liberal party.

A perfect example of the effect of closed primaries and hyper-polarization has on a congressional district is District 8. State Senator Jamie Raskin won the Democrat Primary with 33.6% of the Democrat voters (43,776 votes). But, in reality only 8.9% of the registered voters selected him meaning 91.1% of registered voters (447,930) did NOT vote for the next de facto congressman to represent my home district. This is what partisan gerrymandering with a dollop of closed primaries looks like.

Our Founding Fathers explicitly warned against the dangers of American politics and partisanship. Political parties began to develop during George Washington's first term in office with the Alexander Hamilton's Federalist Party in 1791. The following year, the formation of the Anti-Federalist Party or Democratic-Republicans developed under the leadership of Thomas Jefferson. At the time, this seemed cool because it gave way to the political parties formulating valid views of how government ought to operate in the new republic. But our first president George Washington was fully aware of the dangers of political parties. He viewed the temptation to manifest and retain power as well as revenge of political opponents as the detrimental effects of partisanship. In his farewell address, Washington specifically warned new Americans of the possibilities if political factions gained enough power to obstruct the execution of the laws that were created by Congress and how they could prevent the three branches from properly performing their duties as outlined in the Constitution. Fast forward 300 years or so, sound familiar?!?!

Because today's Republicans and Democrats have sorted themselves into two generally distinct and divergent ideological camps, there tends to be less reaching across party lines as there once was. A few decades ago, one could easily recognize alignments of conservative Republicans and conservative Democrats, and that of liberal Republicans and liberal Democrats. For example, the Civil Rights bills of the 1960s were patched together by Northern Democrats and Republican moderates; they were heavily opposed by Southern Democrats and Republican supporters of states' rights. Like the political atmosphere of now, the fiercest disputes over foreign policy and domestic social equality in the '60s and '70s usually were not between the two parties but *within* them. These days, we are experiencing our own intra-party diversity and discord as voters under the age of 35 have a huge mistrust of government, not fully identifying with either of the two major parties. We cannot emphasize enough the dilemma that hyper-partisanism had on the future of our Republic. If we do not address the divisions now within our electorate, our Republic will deteriorate into a tyrannical oligarchy.

I know this is about becoming a **Born Again Republican**, but I must state, being an independent was extremely liberating. When I stepped out of the Democrat Party last fall, I felt like I could finally breathe and think for myself. The second I clicked off UNAFFILIATED (what you do here in Maryland when you don't register under either party), I immediately began to see the world, at the very least politics, with my own eyes. I would sit there watching debates, and for the first time in my life consider what was being said without party bias. Though I am now a proud Republican, I believe that being an independent voter is the ideal for the sanctity of our country. Independent voters keep the rest of us in check. They can look over the political landscape, and bring a neutral focus. But with closed primaries, being an independent literally relegates you to a second-class citizen. By not being able to participate in primaries, you are stuck with whatever candidate survives to the general. Plus, the voters who do participate in primaries tend to be a lot more of the purist partisans causing the most liberal and the most conservative candidates to become the respective party nominees.

There will always be a part of me that wishes that I could have remained an independent, but running as an indie proved difficult. First, voters are simply used to either D or R, and if that's not confusing enough, there was this new terminology of "unaffiliated" that voters had to learn. We also had to collect 10,000 signatures from registered voters to even appear on the general ballot. That process was quite enjoyable. We encountered the true diversity of voters from across the congressional district. Because we had to interact with residents on a more personal level to collect the information needed for a valid signature, we learned so much from the voters themselves. My team and I got to connect with frustrated residents that wanted to air their grievances and voice their dissatisfaction of government. They felt like no one cares about them anymore. They expressed reasons why they think that money has taken over politics, more importantly that the average voter does not matter anymore. They wondered where are the moderates like them, and there I was standing before them ready to serve. The disturbing connection between displays of hyper-polarization and the erosion of public trust in government is maddening. There is no doubt that voters have less confidence in their elected leaders than they once did. By nearly every available research metric, we can see that public trust in government, and especially in the federal government, has dwindled in the past 20 years. Throughout 2014, Pew Research Center has found that only 19% of Americans express "trust and confidence in government" — the lowest level since 1973. A less obvious question should be asked, how much of this decline can be accredited party behavior, rather than actual competency of public officials? I mean what did we expect voter public opinion of government would be during a heart-wrenching economic crisis, ballooning debt, and two long, inconclusive wars?

While traveling throughout the district and connecting with Carroll and Frederick County voters, what I found immediately interesting was how many voters were unaware of the aforementioned requirements and restrictions that come along with being an Independent or unaffiliated voter. The lack of/presence of voter knowledge is based upon how voters receive information. The growth of "social media" — blogs, cable TV, talk radio — has nurtured the discourse of party politics and their audiences. More voters now obtain virtually all of their information about the world from sources that echo and amplify their ideological predispositions. Most news outlets and political commentators in the mainstream media are partisan talking heads, lamenting the opinion that a more divided Congress is simply a reflection of a more polarized American electorate. This is not true! What the media often fails to educate voters on is the importance of primary elections. We experienced the media bias first hand, and boy are they ruthless. As Chante worked tirelessly trying to break through to local media entities for a possible interview or coverage. The cold shoulder that we received as an Independent only grew more frigid once I became a Republican. For nearly seven months, Chante contacted program producers, managers, hosts, locally and nationwide, through email, phone calls, and social media messages with little to no response. Three weeks away from the Primary, almost every major Democrat candidate had been featured in numerous news articles, featured as guest on radio shows as guests that we contacted BEFORE some had even entered the race. They had the opportunity to reach voters using the same media platforms we previously contacted, and we know this was a tough blow to the campaign. I immediately sprang into action, I logged on to Twitter and started blasting the media for their biases because there is one thing I adapted as a Howard Law graduate: don't mess with my equality. I highlighted the media broadcasts' regulations surrounding Equal Airtime. The "golden rule" stipulates that "radio and television stations and cable systems which originate their own programming must treat legally qualified political candidates equally when it comes to selling or giving away air time." This was not the case at all. It was very obvious that media entities were disenfranchising Maryland voters by dictating who could and couldn't be heard. Chante was told a multitude of excuses that basically said, "We do not have time for ALL candidates just the Democratic candidates." Our campaign was just one of the many that fell victim to the tyranny of the oppressive mainstream media. It came to a point where I even advocated for other non-Democrat candidates to have their voices heard too. It was appalling to me knowing that it is media's job to objectively cover issues that affect their listeners, not stifle the voice of those that are not media and politically elite. Our campaign did not hear back from program producers/managers by the time of the primary. This is one of the many reasons for crafting this book, we wanted to inform voters of how the media is playing an active role in disenfranchising the moderate and more conservative voices across the board, particularly in the DC/Baltimore region.

Here in Maryland, specifically, over 200 years of partisan gerrymandering and election laws (mostly done by Democrats) put the interests of private organizations over the interests of everyday residents and voters. General elections in most of our congressional races are considered non-competitive each and every election year, except this past cycle of course. We've reached a point where the general election is more of a formality rather than an actual process because the system is rigged to favor one major party, the Democrat Party. This is the reason voters were enthusiastic to have another option on the ballot. Residents expressed the importance of electing a leader that is brave and honest. Someone who sees how polarizing our congress has become and is willing to step up and step out to represent their interests first. Not any particular party. What seemed to click with voters the most was the idea that, before we can even get to particular issues, we need to ensure that the process remains accessible to leaders who represent their constituencies completely. But, as time went on, we realized that even when we got on the ballot, we would still have to compete with the major parties and the reality that most voters will mostly just vote for their party's nominees. If I were to have been on the General Ballot, I would have to compete with the Democrat, the Republican, the Green, and the

Libertarian candidate. I eventually decided in the end to not take that risk. If ever you wonder why our electorate and our electeds seem so polarized, it is because it is. It has become virtually impossible for moderates of either party to become elected. We are now at a point whereas, if we do not fix our electoral process, we will never remedy our representatives.

If it were up to me, I would recommend that every new voter should start off as unaffiliated or independent. Voters first vote would not be tainted or encumbered by party loyalty from the beginning, and the voter can evaluate the individual platforms and develop their own values. After they make their first vote and observe how elected officials govern, then they later, if they choose, would determine their party preference. Candidates and parties would become proactive in seeking the support of voters and not just depend on them from blind party loyalty. We would seek the support of voters and not be so concerned about towing the party line. Once all primaries are open, candidates would be forced to break out of their respective factions and our country would have more equitable and representative governance, in my humble opinion.

5 BECOMING AN R

"Whenever human communities are forced to adjust to shifting conditions, pain is ever present."
- John P. Kotter, author of
Leading Change

I remember the night I was approached by a Republican operative to join the party, not only because I thought it was random, but because it was absolutely frigid outside. There we were just wrapping up the 6th District debate in Gaithersburg. I had already got into trouble with the club president for collecting signatures there for my independent race. I had already spent enough time outside the party system that I forgot that my unaffiliated candidacy would eventually go head-to-head with the Republican nominee. "Just think about, Liz. You're really a Republican. You just don't know it yet," the operative said. He was also a young Black millennial, so I was bit curious admittedly. I had already begun to research the Republican Party just before Thanksgiving because I wanted to understand my potential constituency more fully, especially the more conservative parts in the north. I remember clearly the Thanksgiving that my nephew, Henry, said that he was considering becoming a Republican, and I actually said, "I'd rather he be gay. I'd understand that a lot more." So, I was well aware that I had preconceived notions about the GOP. Just like a proper nerd, I went to the library. If anyone is legitimately interested in knowing more about the Republican Party, borrow/buy/read *To Make Men Free: A History of the Republican Party* by Professor Heather Cox Richardson (2014). It breaks down the entirety of the GOP and the complexity of having to balance the two virtues of equality and protection of property. I remember reading the book heading up to visit family in Massachusetts. I recognize now -- reading that one book changed my life.

Joining the party was not easy. I mean the voters and party volunteers were absolutely amazing. There was so much connectivity that it felt like as a Republican I was more American than ever before. I remember the first time I saw the American Flag at a meeting and we pledged it. I've never seen a flag at a Democrat meeting. And, when the Republicans started praying, I remember feeling this peace that I had never felt before. However, I lost A LOT of sleep over becoming a Republican, especially thoughts of being a Black Republican. I am even guilty of laughing at them to their face because I thought they were living oxymorons. I was concerned that people would think I was a RINO. FYI, a RINO is a Republican In Name Only and it is the label that can destroy a person's career just by the mere suggestion. It implies that individual does not stand up to Republican principles, and therefore, should be shunned and degraded. It is also a label that purist use to ostracize moderates in the GOP. One member of the transition team (TransTeam) expressed his excessive concern over it. He was so overzealous that it had become counterproductive. I eventually had to ask him to leave. See, those several weeks I went through the largest

mental and identity shift I had ever undertaken. It was like I had to be ...
Born Again!

Believe me, we hashed it out. Every single aspect of me joining the party, being 2A (for the Second Amendment), having written a blog post the prior fall defending Planned Parenthood, and completing my race as a Republican. We were asking a lot from voters, but we thought that in the end it made more sense. I commend my TransTeam because they pushed me to examine everything. It was during this reflection that I understood I wanted to encourage a Culture of Life. As a Catholic, I remember having to juggle my beliefs as a Christian and the doctrine enforced by my former political party. The last time I participated in activism around abortion was the Hobby Lobby Supreme Court decision. Then, I didn't think anything of it to be pro-abortion. Everyone I knew was, except my mother. Mom and I spoke a lot over the years about her work in women's health as an ob-gyn. I remember asking her what she thought about abortion. She said that as a Catholic, she did not perform them, but would care for the patient in case there was a medical emergency and when complications arouse from abortions. She also told me that a disruption to any pregnancy is a major event, whether it is physical or mental. Becoming a Republican was the first time I honestly began to examine abortion and life. And, after full consideration, that was the first time I would state publicly that I am Pro-Life. Being a Democrat, it is virtually impossible to be Pro-Life anymore. This is some of the concerns that conservative Democrats have. Over the last few years even I could not be 100% Pro-Abortion. The first time I realized the extremism was sitting at a NARAL meeting. I asked the organizer her advice on what I could say to a Christian voter. Her answer was unsatisfactory because she spoke about pregnancy like it was some infectious disease or disorder. There have been a few times where I've been honored to counsel my friends through their decisions to terminate, and I will still be open if need be. I have just witnessed too many pregnancies and anxious parents to ignore the biological, and yes, spiritual amazingness that is birth. Abortionists always push back about rape. I say, what about all these men running around raping women! Why aren't we doing anything about their behavior? Why does everything have to be the fault/burden of women? My father would say that any man that takes advantage of a woman sexually is no man at all. Do something about these weak dudes, and save women and babies from the torment. I take the feminist approach to Life. As a society, we have not done enough to accommodate family, and mothering in particular. Women will not cease being women, and they will continue to live their lives through schooling and work and yes as mothers. Gandhi said, "you can judge a society by how they treat their women." We are decent, but we have a long way to go. I say that all to say, after digging deep, I realized (to my utter astonishment) that I am indeed a conservative.

Once I made the switch, the primary went pretty well. Well, I came in 3rd out of 5, and 2nd in Montgomery County. But, 7,295 Republican voters chose to vote for yours truly, which is not bad for, at that time, a three-month old Republican. I will never forget being up in Westminster (Carroll County) on Primary Day. Per usual, we were greeting voters at the polling locations, and I was surprised that voters were coming up having already decided to vote for me. That was so cool and humbling. Regardless of how the vote turned out, I was so proud of my team and the campaign we had run. I had students from McDaniel and Howard. They got so into it that it was they who got me through the hump. I think voters do want someone more center-right. A lot of them remember

Connie Morella, the Republican congresswoman who served before Van Hollen. It was in her last couple of years that being a "moderate" on Capitol Hill was beginning to be a work hazard, but everywhere we went people still expressed their appreciation for Connie. We wanted to bring back the seat in her honor.

Newsflash: The Republican Party doesn't care about Black People or women either (but for entirely different reasons).

This fact was one of the more difficult notions I had to fathom as a new Republican, and it caused the largest fights between my transition team and me. The conversations went something like this:

> TransTeam: The GOP doesn't care that you're a woman or black woman for that matter.

> Me: Why? Because they are racists, and they don't think that Black women are important? No wonder nobody else wants to be a part of the Republican Party. The country is changing so much, and they better start caring about us, if they want to remain relevant because the train is leaving the station, y'all.

> TransTeam: Why do you make such a big deal about your gender and race anyway? That's what liberals have trained you to think.

> Me: What do you mean? I'm a woman and yes I'm Black. I'm also a daughter of a Filipino immigrant, and yes, my life experiences and heritage are going to be different than some random white dude.

TransTeam: Liz, your race and your gender doesn't matter to Republicans. Stop making such a big deal out of it. If you want to be taken seriously as a Republican, you have to stop making such a big deal out of it.

Me: I'm not making a big deal out of anything. I'm just merely stating I do not and cannot hide who I am. Perhaps, you can, but I'm not going to. If they don't want to accept me for who I am, then perhaps I should have stayed an independent.

TransTeam: Republicans don't care about race or gender because it's not about that. It's about the role of the citizen to its government and that is it. Besides, there is virtually no way you can win as an independent.

It took me a long while to understand what they were trying to tell me, but the core Republican principle stands – **as an American Citizen, your view, your voice is equal to that of any other American Citizen**. It does not matter what color my skin or what gender I identify, I am an American and for the purposes of this country and its future, that is what counts. The Democrat Party has been the main culprit for dividing Americans into factions to pit one kind of person against the other. There is great power in being an American Citizen, and the moment that everyone understands that privilege and right, we will be better off.

This notion that race and/or gender doesn't matter to Republicans has been the hardest one to adjust to. Since I come from some of the most liberal environments ever created like Sidwell, Columbia, and Howard, I find it difficult even for me to move away from race and gender, and trust that I am like everyone else, an individual. For decades, I have been taught that we are different and that we are "other." But, the moment I check back into my full American citizenship, I am reminded of my equitable value. To combat the echoes of inadequacy that liberal teachings have implanted in my conscience, I fight to defend Republicanism and Conservatism as they are rooted in paying righteous honor to God and the preservation of our free society. What made Conservatism feel right to us as a campaign was the ability to provide a more practical, generous and compassionate way to live. Liberalism, although one of the more dominant theories in American Politics, has failed most Black people for the past 50 plus years. With great appreciation to its core values it's important to realize how liberalism is deficient with respect to helping/furthering the understanding of the Black struggle. Liberalism hurts, not helps folks because it does not focus on the individual and considers people just as groups or masses that are easily manipulatable by the emasculating system that is fueled by bias. Once I stepped into the Republican Party and was immediately welcomed for my shared values, I could focus on what we can do to fix the issues in our district as a whole and begin to try to leave behind the identity politics that came from being a former liberal. Greg Gutfeld of PragerU described conservative people as the clean-up crew of America. Once I came to terms and fully understood that it was conservative risk taking that created our civilization, I was confident that we were making the right choice. At the end of the day, Conservatism does not contrast with liberalism, it sustains it.

Now, everything is not all peachy over here in the Republican Party either. I would have to say that racism has no party. You will find bigotry anywhere you go. It's just a matter of what you do in the face of it that makes the difference in the end. Like the time when there was a candidate forum at Leisure World during the 2016 Primary. Right before the election took place, our campaign realized that we did not receive an invitation to connect with Republican voters at the largest retirement community and voting region in Montgomery County. The voting population of Leisure World is so large and significant that it has two voting precincts assigned to it. We decided to attend the last candidate forum so that the residents knew that we were interested in their concerns. But when we arrived, we were met with hostility. I wasn't expecting what happened next. The head of the club admitted that he met me a couple of months back and purposefully decided not to invite me to connect with his chapter. Perhaps it was my faith or naivete, but I wasn't expecting such ill will. He invited each of the other candidates, and he even invited someone who did not register to run in the end. This man was looking at me with such disgust. I can remember just standing there looking at the members of the club. They looked back at me, and asked that I be able to participate, but the president refused. I suppose he had the only say. He initially he said I could introduce myself at the beginning of the event, but then later said he "changed [his] mind and asked that I just sit in the back of the room and don't say a word." It took every bone in my body, all the faith in God I had, and the strength of my ancestors not to break down in front of everyone that evening. Again, I admit I have been spared these humiliating situations until I hit adulthood, but when you experience the venom of racism, it doesn't take that long to feel its effects. How I wished I had not brought James, one of my Howard intern, up with me. I felt badly to have exposed him to this aspect of our community or the stereotype of my new party, but I was also grateful that he was there with me because I don't think I would have survived that moment alone. I could think of no other reason why the president did not want me, except for something so unspeakable as the prejudice and contempt that he had for my very being. Oddly, that was the only reason that made sense considering the circumstances. I knew what it was, but quite frankly, I was not expecting it at all.

I try my hardest not to think that situations like these are racist or bigoted, but there is sort of this eerily innate feeling that starts somewhere deep within my heart that swells to the surface and causes this intense panic like I imagine an allergic reaction would feel like. Racism and bigotry are like toxins to the soul. All the more reason we need anecdotes. I would then go back to the power of liberty and individualism (and God of course!). Standing earnestly in the power of our individuality, no one can break you down especially when living fully in your citizenship and living with grace. I see us as a people finding issue with executing this sort of higher way of being. We forget (somewhat easily) that there is this responsibility to ourselves, to society, and to God. The problem with Secularism is it eradicates our focal point, our common anchor, our common responsibility. When you take the focus from God and place it directly and solely on society, you place too much power on mutability. Secularism also removes the responsibility of the individual and places supreme power on the State. In this country in particular, the State was never supposed to be made more powerful than the citizenry. The moment we honor our individualism, we will begin to force racism to dissipate. The government's only purpose was to preserve the liberty and freedoms of the individual. When we relinquish our constitutional principles to the State, we cease to be Americans.

6 WHAT IS A CONSERVATIVE ANYWAY?

**"A creative man is motivated by the desire to achieve,
not by the desire to beat others."**

– Ayn Rand

Don't worry. I didn't understand what a conservative was until a year ago either. Like most Democrats, I looked at conservatives with a worrisome stare. Granted, anything I knew about conservatives or the Conservative Movement, I knew from other democrats or from mainstream media, mainly CNN or MSNBC. From what I heard, I didn't think that Conservatism was for me, but since my congressional district was half-conservative, I thought it was a good thing to know more about my people. I quickly found out that it can be a lot to take in at first, but once you understand a few basic concepts, you too may find out that you're a conservative too!

The place I like to start is the term. In the political context, conservatives believe in conserving the Republic. We always refer to what Benjamin Franklin said when asked what kind of government did the founders create, **"A Republic, if you can keep it."** Conservatives believe that it is our responsibility as American Citizens to do our part to conserve the Republic. Now, the thing about Conservatism is that since the philosophy involves the individual citizen, the prescription of Conservatism varies from individual-to-individual from what I have noticed. When I asked about it, I have never received the same answer twice. There is a formula to Conservatism and the individual takes his portion to manifest what Conservatism means to that particular citizen. So, here are the ingredients:

Freedom

Faith

Family

&

Free Enterprise

Being a conservative is to believe in the **American Dream** - every citizen can tap into your God-given potential and thrive. Regardless of how you were born or where you came from, here in this country, when you are industrious, self-reliant, and yes, spiritual, you can prosper. Immigrants understand the American Dream specifically because they have left their home country for a better life. When my mother came to this country at the age of 25, her mother told her to go to America and not come back. She said that because she knew that the opportunities in the states were exponentially greater than those in the Philippines, especially for her daughters. So, when my mother became an American Citizen when I was a year old, she did so with immense love for the country that allowed her to forge her prosperous future. My father's life also follows this American Dream as a native. You witness the possibility of American **freedom** when you consider how my father's progression from E. St. Louis to Washington flows to American Prosperity through education, dedication, and calling.

But for my generation and for this current era, The American Dream seems like an aberration, particularly for native born Americans. Whether they live in the North or South, in the cities or on farms, true advancement remains dubious. For our Republic to endure the rapid changes and population growth, we need to reignite and honor our citizenship. The American Citizen was crafted to be the strongest citizen in history. Before we declared our independence from British Rule and before our constitution was crafted, actual rulers controlled the lives and the trajectory of every human being on the planet. Sure, parliamentary governance existed, but power remained in the hands of the elite and landed gentry. By establishing our Constitutional Republic, our Founders constricted the powers of the government to secure the blessings of Individual Liberty.

For the ultimate primer to understand the relationship of the American Citizen to the State, refer to *The Conscience of a Conservative* by Senator Barry Goldwater. In 1960, he laid out the rationale for conservative principles, and the theories ring eerily true to this day. The ultimate warning of Conservatism is that government has been throughout history "the chief instrument for thwarting man's liberty." The view of government is that it is "power in the hands of some men to control and regulate the lives of other men." Goldwater focused on the "omnipresence of government." He warns about the growth of the government getting so great that it becomes a "leviathan" or behemoth that is "out of touch with the people and out of their control." Goldwater stated that the current understanding in society is that everyone should be brought down to a common level and that individual success is demonized. Right now, our government has never been so powerful and citizens been so insecure about their potential.

After you read Goldwater, I suggest you read anything written by Jack Kemp, the former congressman from New York State, Housing and Urban Development Secretary under George H.W. Bush, Vice Presidential running mate of Bob Dole in 1996, quarterback for the Buffalo Bills, and former trustee of Howard University. Full disclosure, I befriend his son, Jimmy, during and after the primary (and he endorsed me!). Jimmy Kemp leads The Jack Kemp Foundation to continue to champion "The American Idea" that he says is both "a birthright and an obligation." I remember the hours Chante and I spent in the campaign office reading through Congressman Kemp's words. We were like, Yassss! I mean his words rang so true for both of us; we totally geeked out. He spoke about why **faith and family** must remain central to our lives. Not in an overbearing or judgmental way, but how they relate to social order. He believed that our society puts "the center of decision-making power neither with the individual nor with the government, but somewhere in between - in the family, the church, and the community." If you take an honest moment to look at how you live your life, you will see the pillars that keep you straight. For me, I've already told you how important my family is to me and my worldview. Though I can always be a better human and Catholic, I have felt what it is like to both distrust and believe in God. It is somewhat difficult to explain, but it basically comes down to the soul. I believe everyone has a soul (and some religions believe all living things have one). But, you are basically a soul in this body for this lifetime charged to navigate through time. How faith plays out in our country is that it is supposed to guide us through our lives and helps us interact with one another. Does our country need a reset, absolutely! Unfortunately, faith and "religious people" get a bad rap these days, but when this country was formed, the founders would have never considered creating a God-less Republic. They just didn't want one particular religion to rule. So many other countries were/are controlled by a specific religion and hinder the freedom of their citizens. Nevertheless, faith shepherds our way.

The last element to Conservatism may be the most difficult to comprehend in present day - **Free Enterprise**.

Free enterprise is basically the ability to transact and compete in the marketplace free of interference from the State. Obviously, just like communism and socialism, there has never been absolute free market capitalism. But unlike other forms of society, capitalism remains the only kind that accepts higher quality of life and cultivates happiness. Again, consider the spectrum of power, either the individual has control or the State or somewhere in between. Laws, taxes, and regulations can guide (or control) the behavior within and among ventures, but the free market germinates best practices through competition. Ideally, businesses compete to sell to interested consumers. If you have the better product, service, price, then the market will respond in your favor. When taxes and regulations balloon; however, the system bogs down business, and freedom/creativity/innovation/well-being suffers.

These days, folks have such a perverted view of capitalism, and there is a growing movement to reject it all together. But, conservatives believe the alternative is caustic to the Republic because again, back to freedom, the more the State controls the less the individual does. People then relinquish power. Collectivists want everyone to be subordinate to the State, and the Welfare State is the tool used for said subjugation according to Senator Goldwater. People often think that conservatives are heartless creeps, but this Welfare State that we abhor is not welfare, it is the overblown system that enslaves both the recipient and the taxpayer. The bigger Government grows the smaller the individual citizen becomes. A contemporary composition that breaks down the limitless power of free enterprise would be *The Conservative Heart: How to Build a Fairer, Happier, and More Prosperous America* by Arthur C. Brooks, the president of the American Enterprise Institute. Brooks's formula emphasizes "meaningful work" as key to happiness. (Remember, Life, Liberty and the Pursuit of Happiness? That happiness.) He believes that "free enterprise empowers us" to choose our lives. We have a "moral obligation to give every American a better shot at living a happy and meaningful life," according to Brooks. Our overgrown system now encourages "soul-crushing dependence" on the state while bastardizing liberating work.

Capitalism is not the problem; however, it is crony-capitalism. In a nutshell, crony-capitalism is the absolute perversion of our government and capitalism. Big corporations pay big money to prop up elected officials and influence policies that protect them against competition. It is this crony-capitalism that gives capitalism a bad name. No other economic system has fostered more prosperity and creativity than capitalism. Government's role should only exist to set basic parameters to prevent bad people from doing bad things. Limited government focused on equal protection is the only way we can conserve free enterprise and honest competition. Over-bloated government, complicated tax policy, and protectionist regulations epitomize crony-capitalism. The cost to society is great. Instead of allowing for innovation, competition, and diversity, our economy shrinks leaving a handful of cronies and limited options for consumers and employees. The extreme lack of jobs and hopelessness that Americans feel is directly related to crony-capitalism.

The flip-side of this crony-capitalism is limited government. You may hear us conservatives champion a reduction of government spending or reducing the National Debt while rejecting burdensome taxes and regulations, particularly on businesses. These concepts are related back to individualism and freedom. We do not work to feed the government coffers; the government is to provide for the general welfare and apportion tax money mindfully. The government has grown so large from crony-capitalism, it has basically made citizenship a burden. When we take a sober evaluation of our spending, identify what is necessary and recalibrate, we will have the means to mend the pervasive concerns.

As you can tell, Conservatism is a philosophy that helps individuals navigate how best they can pursue opportunity and conserve the Republic. In my humble opinion, I believe that Conservatism will serve the overall community better than liberalism because it creates a space of value and possibility. The way that liberalism has manifested is despair. The main issue of Conservatism is that it needs more people to participate and different people to bear witness to its merits for the formula to truly benefit the Republic for which it seeks to conserve.

If you do have a dream, the best way you make sure it's a reality is you gotta start at the bottom. You have to start at the bottom, and just work your way up. Because along the way, you're gonna learn it from A to Z. And it's not gonna be easy. You're gonna go through periods where you're unsure if this is the right path you were supposed to take, but eventually you're gonna break through. And you're gonna find your way. At least, you've built a foundation for yourself where as though you can stand on your own two.

– Marion Christopher Barry

(6/17/80 – 8/14/16)

7 IF YOU REALLY THINK THAT #BLACKLIVESMATTER, THEN SUPPORT THE REPUBLICAN RENAISSANCE...FOR THE REPUBLIC...OR ELSE

"The Republican Party would not even exist except for black Americans. Our party was born out of the struggle for equality and opportunity - the two always went together."

- Jack Kemp

I believe the worst thing that Black people have ever done to our country was to divorce ourselves from the Republican Party. Since the death of Lincoln in 1865, African Americans had been loyal followers of the Republican Party. Despite their faithfulness, black northern politicians had never received political rewards equal to the value of the African-American vote to the GOP. The informal and unwritten Compromise of 1877 was a clear indication the Republican Party had neglected the African American community. To decide a disputed election of 1876, both political parties met up in a downtown Washington DC hotel to discuss the terms of the presidency. Tilden and the Democrat Party accepted a GOP victory with Rutherford Haynes, if GOP pledges were upheld. Many of the terms dictated would directly overturn progress for newly freed slaves. President Ulysses Grant sent National Guard troops into the south to assist with reconstruction and protect the new citizens of America. The compromise asked Northern Republicans to withdraw federal troops from the five military district in the former Confederacy, effectively ending Reconstruction. They wanted all assistance given to freed men to cease immediately, and lastly, they wanted economic assistance, from the industrialized North to rebuild the South. With the departure of the army, Republican governments in the South toppled as former slaves were prevented from voting by using crafty legal maneuvers, sometimes covert, but often outright intimidation and terrorism. Loss of the Black vote was quickly followed by segregation laws and other discrimination against Blacks.

Divorcing ourselves from the Republican Party and choosing the Democrat Party degraded the success of everyone. Robert Lee Vann helped serve the divorce papers in the 1930s — the decade when black voters first began to flee the Republican Party, then known as the "Party of Lincoln," an ideological home so very different from what "Republican" means today. As *The Pittsburgh Courier's* editor and publisher, under his leadership he helped develop it into one of the nation's leading Black newspapers. Under Vann's guidance the *Courier* called for improvements for African Americans in areas such as housing, education, and health care. A primary goal of the *Courier* was to empower Blacks both economically and politically. Articles and editorials encouraged the Black community's support of organizations such as The National Association for the Advancement of Colored People and The National Urban League. Vann was heavily involved with politics during his association with The Courier. Initially a Republican, he grew disillusioned with the party and converted to the Democrat Party. Sixty-seven years after Lincoln's assassination, Vann declared "the debt has been paid in full." Although Pennsylvania was one of six states to vote for Herbert Hoover in 1932, that election marked the beginning of the exodus of African Americans from the Republican Party. On September 11, 1932, Vann delivered a famous speech at the St. James Literary Forum in Cleveland, Ohio entitled "The Patriot and the Partisan." This speech, although rarely mentioned in history, was monumental in the shift towards liberalism in the African American community. Vann urged African American voters throughout the nation to turn away from the Republican Party which had failed them, and support the Democrat Party of Franklin D. Roosevelt in the 1932 election. Vann claimed that "the only true gauge by which to judge an individual or a party or a government is not by what is proclaimed or promised, but by what is done... In those years, the early years of Reconstruction, when Negroes held the highest offices, the literacy of the Negro was only ten percent. Today [back then], the literacy of the Negro in this country is eighty-four percent and yet the same Republican Party not only declares the Negro unfit to hold office but organizes Lily-Whitism as an excuse and justification for keeping Negroes out of office...." He fully recognized the political weight of the minority vote, which is why he introduced the idea of "Loose Leaf Politics."

Vann believed that it was wrong that Blacks had to wait until a political faction addressed their concerns before they gave up their support. He was the father of all flip-floppers, but with excellent reason. He argued if we present our interests to both parties without definite allegiance to one in particular, then BOTH parties would have to succumb to the needs their African American electorate. Vann stated,

"The only true political philosophy that dictates the Negro to select his party, is the austerity that we cannot wait to be selected." Converging African American voters into Democrats was not an easy task, but it was one Robert Vann was dedicated to supporting up until his death. It was with this speech, that was later published that he got millions of African American voters to turn the picture of Lincoln to the wall and vote a Democrat ticket. He proudly proclaimed "I, for one, shall join the ranks of this new army of fearless, courageous, patriotic Negroes who know the difference between blind partisanship and patriotism." The successful election of Franklin D. Roosevelt was mostly in part by Vann's bitterness with the GOP and his leadership with Roosevelt's Colored Advisory Committee. Vann's support of the Democrat Party also thrust him upon the national stage. In 1935, FDR appointed the former tobacco worker from North Carolina to be the nation's first Black assistant attorney general. As the depression dragged on, Vann became more and more disappointed with both the federal and state New Deal programs. To keep the support of southern Democrats, FDR permitted the segregation of New Deal work relief programs and accepted gross inequalities in provision of aid. In 1938, when Vann and other African American leaders called for an end to racial discrimination in the military, the Roosevelt administration remained silent on that issue.

Disappointed with the slow pace of change, Vann again changed his political allegiance and backed Republican Wendell Wilkie in the 1940 presidential election. However, Vann's death in 1940 would seal the fate of the black vote in the Democrat Party forever. Vann's disillusionment with the Democrat Party, however, was not shared by all. During the Great Depression, Pennsylvania's black voters, after unwavering allegiance to the party of Lincoln since the 1860s, made the great transition into the Democrat Party. In Philadelphia, a new generation of African American leaders, including Reverend Marshall Lorenzo Shepard, Raymond Pace, Robert N. C. Nix, and Crystal Bird Faucet mobilized black voters to stay in the party of the Roosevelts. With that effort, they won elected offices, and led the revitalized struggle against racial discrimination. Many Black Pennsylvanians, like African Americans across the country, felt a deep admiration for FDR, who opened the doors of opportunities unseen since early Reconstruction. But black empowerment leaders, such as Vann and others quickly discovered, FDR's upward mobility of Blacks was oftentimes seen as "window dressing". This would lead to his disenchantment with his new party, and a new call to action. It is safe to say that once we mobilized our vote towards the Democrat Party, it was immediately locked down by the presumptuous *New Deal*, and further kept under lock and key with Lyndon B. Johnson's Great Society.

As I track the timeline of the black conservative vote, there is this lingering notion that we lost ourselves when we gave up Conservatism. Everyone should exercise his or her full citizenship, and returning to conservative principles will allow more of us to succeed. The American Citizen is the most powerful citizen in the history of history. As a newly minted conservative, I would like to explain my stance and how our citizenship is significant considering the glacial shift that has occurred in Black America, especially regarding America's role in the world. A consequence of the Civil Rights Movement and the Black Power ideology in the 1960s was a growing identification of Black Americans with other oppressed peoples around the world. This has had less to do with a common skin color and more to do with shared social and political subjugation caused by common colonizers. Many Blacks sympathize with Asian workers and Northern Irish Catholics (despite problematic Asian-Black and Irish-Black relations in places like California and Boston respectively). More and more Blacks became cognizant of how South Africa oppressed its native peoples. In fact, the radical consequences for domestic issues of this growing international consciousness only deepen the global understanding for equality.

The real issue that faces our country is that some people view fellow Americans as less than. As a new Republican, I recognize how beneficial honest public discourse would be to highlight the breakdown of the moral fabric in the country and create sustainable solutions, especially for the people who have struggled the most. Cornel West revealed the rationale behind the black conservative and acknowledged the decline of values such as patience, hard work, deferred gratification and self-reliance that then gives rise to high crime rates, the increasing number of unwed mothers, and the relatively uncompetitive academic performances of young people. In addition, it goes without saying that we must examine the prevalence of secularization, hyper-sexualization, and violence used by the mass media and how advertisers often deployed them to coax and seduces certain groups of consumers or by the "entertainment" industry to manipulate behavior.

The economic boom of Post-World War II created new strategies to generate general consumption, secularization-- especially aimed at American youth projecting sexual activity as instant gratification and violence as the expression of masculine identity. This market activity has contributed greatly to the disorientation and confusion of American youth and those with less education and fewer opportunities. They bear the brunt of this cultural chaos. Should we be surprised that black youths isolated from the labor market, marginalized by decrepit urban schools, devalued by alienating ideals of beauty and targeted by an unprecedented drug invasion exhibit high rates of crime and teenage pregnancy?

By giving away our Republicanism, we gave up on our collective dignity, integrity, and our complete citizenship. There is no better time than the present to reclaim what is technically our birthright.

8 FIVE REASONS WHY I ACTUALLY DO SUPPORT TRUMP FOR PRESIDENT
BY THE WAY, MY TRANSITION HAS EVERYTHING AND NOTHING TO DO WITH TRUMP
AND FINALLY, THE TRUMP FACTOR IS THE OPPOSITE OF THE WILDER EFFECT

"Curiouser and curiouser!" Cried Alice (she was so much surprised, that for the moment she quite forgot how to speak good English)."
- Alice's Adventures in Wonderland &
Through the Looking-Glass by Lewis Carroll

If everything works out, this book will be published before the results of the 2016 Presidential Election are revealed. So, when I speak of the Trump Factor, I am speaking prior to said election results revelation and before the pundits have at it. If the man loses, the dye is cast, but if he wins, I can say, I told you so.

Practically every person I speak to either can't stand Donald Trump or won't admit planning to vote for Donald Trump, which is the case for most Republicans in my region. Now, I openly and unapologetically admit that I will vote for the man. First, you can't blame me. I was a Kasich supporter during the primary, and he actually won in the county I live in. I believe that ever since the beginning of the primary, Governor Kasich was the best challenge to Hillary Clinton and therefore would not be supported through the primary by The Establishment. But despite losing my best friend from college over this election, I support Donald J. Trump because of what I have experienced personally.

Reason Number One: He is challenging the status quo.

I know for a fact that Hillary Clinton was promised the White House by the Powers That Be the moment that Barack Obama became the Democrat nominee in 2008. Forget backroom deals, Hillary's concession was not the State Department. That was just the first course. 2016 was her *piece de resistance*. Just think about it. Hillary had minimal challenge from the Democrat establishment. Former Governor Martin O'Malley may be the most "progressive" governor to ever govern over the state of Maryland. Under his administration, we got gay marriage, transgender rights, offshore wind energy, AND the end to the death penalty. With all that, he only managed to get 1% in Iowa. **Bollocks.** I call conspiracy theory on that one. Plus, the man is gorgeous, young, sings Rock & Roll, and plays the guitar. The challenger the Establishment did not consider was Independent (democrat-socialist, whatever) Bernie Sanders. I mean. If the universe wasn't conspiring to stop someone's ascension to the presidency first with a young, charismatic, handsome, and tall Black man named Barack Obama, then next time around you throw a unapologetically leftist, rabble-rouser, doozy of a candidate like Bernie Sanders! You cannot make this stuff up.

Zero opposition came from the Democrat Party. Hillary's challenger came from the nosebleed section left of left field.

I support Mr. Trump because he, like I, was willing to take on The Establishment. Most people who come through the rank and file of either political party have been indoctrinated into a particular way of thinking, which boils down to seek permission or don't rock the boat if you care about your political future. When you care more about the future than your own political career, you tend to fight even harder for the truth. You see what's hamstringing the system and you believe and you are willing to do something about it. As I did, so has Trump.

Technically, I have had a longer political career than Trump has, which is truly outrageous, but true. With every blunder he makes, I feel for him because I know firsthand what it is like to be new to the world of politics. You never know how brutal politics can be until to you personally step into the ring. I don't care if it's for school board, president, or dogcatcher, the amount of exposure, scrutiny, criticism, all these eyeballs on you. The moment you become a candidate, especially one that is a strong challenger to the status quo, you cease to be your own person any longer. As hard as you fight, you no longer can define yourself. As hard as you may try, everyone else will create an opinion about you, even in a moment. Whether at a community event or from something stated in the media, once the person formulates that view of you, it is near impossible to change that perception. When you know that this happens at a harsher extend when you challenge The Establishment, and you are willing to do it anyway because you believe it is the right thing to do for your community and the future, then good on you.

Reason Number Two: Being Called a Racist Sucks

Speaking of perceptions. The worst possible one is being considered a racist. Unfortunately, even I have been called a racist, by the now former Fox News Anchor Greta Van Susteren no less. Before we go any further, Black people cannot be considered racists because racism (and race) is a social construct created by the powerbrokers of society to control the masses by dividing them into factions so they would not band together and upend the feeble hold on Society by The Powerful. In this country, throughout our history, the people who have traditionally wielded power over the rest of society do tend to be white men with copious resources and expendable wealth. Historically, these fellow Americans were Democrats who fought tooth and nail to ensure that poor Whites and freed Blacks would never unify to take on and challenge their establishment. Whether they were riot busters or petition line breakers, similarly situated working class Americans have been pitted against each other and made to think that they were each other's enemies, when in fact, if only they realized their commonality, they might realize their own capacity for power. For Blacks (or any non-white person) to be considered racists, they would have to be in a position of power to manipulate others into submission. Since this is not the case, then I cannot be racist. Besides, as a person of mixed heritage, many different cultures make up my family; hence, every one of them influenced my point of view and through this blended identification, I am naturally more empathetic in my interactions.

Nevertheless, with one news article, I was called a racist when I called out one of the Democrat candidates for being out of touch with the rest of us. So, here's what happened. One evening I was scheduled to talk with law students over at Howard Law when I got word that there was a non-partisan candidate forum held by a bunch of environmentalist groups. I had not heard one peep about it before that evening, and as a registered candidate at that time, I believed that I should have had the same opportunity to connect with voters as the Democrat candidates that were invited seeing that it was a non-partisan event and all. Just democrat candidates were invited to participate (they received the invitation weeks prior). Not a single Republican nor I were invited to attend. It is actually unlawful for non-profit groups to hold partisan events. So, I crashed it. When I walked into the Silver Spring Civic Center, it was packed as I knew that it would be. There was many a familiar face in the room, so I expected the organizers to recognize me. There was this guy (he was "that" guy, in charge but clueless). I tell you. Not only did he give me some lame excuse about all registered candidates were invited (I pulled up on my phone my registration from the month prior to call him out on his b.s.), but he also had the gall to ask if the candidate was present. I'm the bloody candidate, you moron! This guy and I both ran for the same position a year prior. We saw each other no less than 25 times throughout the course of the primary, but right then and there I realized, he did not see me as an individual. Or perhaps he could not register that someone like me would be a candidate. I have no clue, but that infuriating interaction just pushed me over the edge. So, by the time this clown gave me permission to participate in the panel, I was livid.

I didn't expect the first candidate-to-candidate question to come to me. After all, I wasn't even supposed to be there, so when Kathleen Matthews (old local news anchor and wife of the notorious Chris Matthews from MSNBC) asked me a direct question, I was rather surprised. Her question to me went something like this, "In your opinion, do you think gender is important when considering voting for this position, now that we are losing Barbara Mikulski in our congressional delegation?" When I heard Mikulski, I thought she was talking about the Senate race, and I said that one should vote for the person who would best represent and serve the people, and that it shouldn't matter about that person's gender. Well, Kathleen Matthews then goes onto to say something along the lines of "women are woefully underrepresented in Congress and the boardroom, I think it's very important when considering our next congressperson" (to this day I don't know why that became her drug of choice…woefully…who says woefully anyway). I asked her how is she going to represent our district in Congress now that she is a minority. She cited that women make up the majority of this district. And then I pointed to the two other women running for the same position (Ana Sol Gutierrez and myself). I mean with the district as it is now as a millionaire white woman, how do you expect to represent the rest of us. And with those three words "millionaire white woman," I was branded a racist. Here is the problem with all of that. When I tell you Kathleen Matthews has no clue, I mean she doesn't. I don't care what her race is, she lives in a bubble, and I would know since I'm one of the few who tried to break out of it the moment I knew what was up. Because of the redistricting rich people like Kathleen Matthews are a small, but concentrated portion of our congressional district. As such they are out of touch with the remainder of the district and that's a simple fact. She was wrong on two fronts. 1) When she speaks about the diversity of our county she thinks it is because of a new influx of immigrants. She does not consider the decades of redlining and discriminatory practices of homeowners, realtors, and banks to prohibit Black people from living in white neighborhoods. She does not acknowledge her ability to take advantage of the GI bill from her father's service was not afforded to many of her non-white contemporaries. By not receiving the same earned benefit, non-white contemporaries had a more difficult task of ascending to a higher economic class to gain the generational or expendable wealth that she was afforded. 2) Kathleen and quite a number of people use the word women and think white women. When she continuously campaigned about her being a woman when she knew full well that she was running against two other women, she negated our womanhood. She wasn't the only woman in the race, and she had no right to disregard us like she most certainly and consistently did for self-promotion. Kathleen Matthews has not experienced a scintilla of what Ana Sol Gutierrez or I have, so she was wrong to claim that our experiences would not be just as beneficial to the House of Representatives (and I would argue our insight would benefit the district more considering the demographic makeup of the district and the country at large). So, Greta Van Susteran and her Internet trolls can call me racist all they want, but the truth still stands, I was correct in calling Kathleen Matthews out for her obliviousness.

So, when I see Donald Trump taking on one of Kathleen Matthews bosom buddies, Hillary, I know exactly why he is so amped up. It is extremely infuriating to interface with elitist liberals who claim to care about everyone else, when we all know full well they could care less about anyone who isn't a part of their clique. I am hard on The Democrat Party simply because it is the one that professes to defend the downtrodden when you realize it is government policies that repress the average citizens economic progress and personal growth. Besides I have been told that by running for Congress, I was acting like a white man. I know, people say the craziest things to me. It definitely makes me wonder if these sorted statements are spoken to men? or people of less melanin? I have no idea, but the guy who said that went on to say that only white men in this country get to step out and take the sort of ballsy move I took over the course of last year. Isn't that the exact sort of equality that y'all strived for in the 60s, you know, Dr. King's content of our character dream stuff. Perhaps when faced with the reality of equality, some folks are just not ready even though we are passing the second-generation mark already.

Reason Number Three: The Democrat Party doesn't listen to voters anyway

This is another harsh criticism of my former party I know, but I cannot begin to tell you how frustrated voters have become with practically everything. I suppose time will tell from the General Election whether voters will actually act on their frustration, but even from the Baltimore County Field Office, I could tell that voters had enough. We spent countless days calling into more rural parts of the state in 2014. The Democrat Party assumed that Baltimore, Anne Arundel, and Frederick counties were far enough into the hinterlands that they did not bother to fully commit to campaigning in the other half of the state. To their detriment, they focused 75% of their campaigning efforts in Prince George's, Montgomery, and Baltimore City assuming that the high concentration of Democrat votes would push them over the edge. They were only focused on the numbers, and they weren't much concerned with connecting to actual voters.

As one of the alternative counties, we were responsible for calling "the others", and virtually every caller we heard from said that

Larry Hogan would be the first Republican they would be voting for. Oh, did I mention we were only calling registered Democrats. Self-proclaimed lifelong Democrats decried that they felt like they were not being heard. The economic downturn hit families and communities hard across the state. If they had a job, they were one of the lucky ones. Senior citizens who wanted to retire could not because they had to support their grandchildren after their own children lost their jobs. Many middle-aged residents hit hard financial times, got divorced, and some moved back in with their parents. The economic downturn was brutal and the recovery was too slight. All these calls, all this pain was relayed to the main office and their response was "democrats don't poll well with economic messages." Well, why doesn't someone change the messaging! Perhaps it's because they don't have any good solid solutions to fix the economy. They only can offer more government programs, and feel good rhetoric. But, as James Carville said, "It's the Economy, stupid." I support Trump because of my firsthand account of how tone deaf the Democrat Party was to the voices of the average voters. I do believe that Mr. Trump has an authentic concern for everyone's economic plight. Just like I became fed up with the endless excuses, so had Donald Trump. I commend him for stepping out of his comfort zone and standing up for the rest of us.

Reason Number Four: Liberal Intimidation is A Weapon of Hate

Apart from September 11th, I've never been so afraid in my life than being a new Republican. I suppose I should feel lucky that I have lived a rather safe life, but I think I'm getting to know what hate feels like and now it's coming directly from classmates and people who I thought were friends. At first it was just at the polling locations during last spring's primary. Usually, when you are out, you try to connect voters, try to hand out literature, and if they are not interested, they simply say, "no, thank you." But, the moment we say the word, Republican, quite a few comments immediately turn into jeers. It was so bad that even my dear mother noticed. One afternoon during Early Voting, I picked Mom up from her polling location. Even as we were rushing back and forth, I noticed that something was different about her. I asked her if anything was wrong and she shared with me the following story:

"Liz, today I got a little upset. You know, I was doing my usual routine, as I was passing your literature out, I approached a lady and said, 'can you please vote for my daughter, she's running for Congress.' She took your flyer and when she saw that you were a Republican, she threw it back in my face. I was so shaken, and you know she was an African-American woman!"

I felt so sorry for my mom; her joy was met with so much negativity. Unfortunately, those sorts of interactions have become somewhat routine, and yes, particularly when interacting with other African American women. Remember when I said that Black women are the most loyal Democrat voting block, unfortunately, we have fallen for the gambit that the Democrat Party has sold us hook, line, and sinker. We as a people are extremely loyal and opinionated, but it is very interesting to experience the visceral rejection of another human being, and yes, another Black woman, simply because I identify as a Republican. I believe 100% that a liberal's understanding of Republicans and Conservatism only comes from other liberals' defining us as the boogeyman and whackos. With that preconception, liberals hold onto their myopic view and disparage anything and everyone that opposes their adamant worldview.

Attacking the opposition is actually a well-backed organizing tactic cultivated by Saul Alinsky, the man who inspired both Hillary Clinton and Barack Obama. Alinsky's violent tactics have been so successful in society that they have become second-nature to liberals and most don't know they are using them. Take Rule #5 as an example: "Ridicule is man's most potent weapon". Or, Rule #11: "If you push a negative hard and deep enough it will break through into its counterside; this is based on the principle that every positive had its negative." You have seen plenty of this throughout this election year, but the hardest ridicule has come in the last month leading up to the election. In my view, the personal attacks are last ditch efforts as if there is desperation coming from the Democrat Party. Alinsky uses the term "enemy" to explain his radicalizing tactics, and insists that the polarization, the Us v. Them, the "if you're not with us then you're against us" mentality is necessary to force the radical change sought. I do not have to go farther than my own Facebook page to see examples of this negativism tactic. Because I support Trump, and before that, when I became a Republican, "friends" call me an idiot, crazy, that I've "lost it", and they even question my blackness. One man called me a traitor, and another man even delighted at my losing two elections and called me ignorant.

Social media has its benefits, but the greatest downside is that it has given users a way to tap into their nastiest self. Because they can type any old thing from the safety of their space with no regard to the recipient's feelings, they type whatever they want. Contemptuous comments are made public, and because of that the negativity is magnified. Negative comments on Facebook feel like they seep into your conscience to a point that it feels like you cannot escape the evil. I do believe that all the attacks on Facebook have something to do with the ridicule tactic. Some folks are genuinely curious about my point of view, but for the most part, so called friends are not interested in understanding, they only care about defending their beliefs by attacking mine. They hit so hard because they are afraid that we may be right after all. Alinsky said that "the real action is in the enemy's reaction." I do believe that the comments flung at me are not for dialogue purposes, but to ridicule and harm. The aim is to destroy. The goal is to silence. With every negative comment, I receive from a Democrat even if they are friends, I realize now that this is the mentality that has been forged---As a **Born Again Republican**, I am now their enemy.

Regardless of what Trump has done or hasn't done, both he and I are now out of the liberal pack and have become its prey. Because of this I would rather stand by Trump than cower to liberal intimidation.

Reason Number Five: Now I know what Media Bias Looks Like

You have probably heard a lot about the Liberal Media or Media Bias. I thought it was a hoax too until I experienced it myself last year. I have already spoken about the time when I was an independent and because I pointed out the obliviousness of another candidate who is in fact a "millionaire white woman," I was branded a racist for days. But, the moment I joined the Republican Party, I realized that the media actually turns a blind eye if not myopic one to non-democrat candidates. The other media markets may be different, but when you look at the Washington market, you begin to see how large the liberal lore looms. Take the good old Washington Post. To cover the congressional primaries, they chose to write individual articles on seven of the nine democrat candidates. They even wasted ink on a kitschy "5 things to know about..." piece covering the lot of them. And, after all of that, The Washington Post writer placed all five Republican candidates into one article entitled, "One Conservative and Four Moderates". You can probably guess which candidate won the Republican nomination. From the coverage of the Republican Primary for congress you can begin to see where the media bias/agenda/control begins. When pushed, reporters will say, "it's the editor's or producer's choice" or even better "it's not like a Republican can win this seat anyway." News Channel 8's Bruce DePuyt is the only reporter that changed his initial no to a yes and had me on air to talk about the campaign (and for that, I will never forget him). When there is less coverage of anything, there is less attention obviously. The Washington Press treats our region like it's 100% Liberal when there is absolutely more diversity than that. And since they are national Press if they treat our region this way, you can imagine the treatment they give to "Fly Over Nation." We are just ignored and the perception proliferates.

If traditional media coverage is that limited at the local or congressional level, I now do not give it much credit for delivering honest information to help voters make informed decisions. The media now steers voters in the direction that only it approves of and ignores/rejects the rest. And when you add Reason 4 to Reason 5, you get the main reason why I support Donald Trump. Now, I really don't trust a word mainstream media says because they have a nefarious agenda.

Finally: Trump Factor is the Opposite of the Wilder Effect

Again, time will tell, but I do believe that people are not being honest when asked who they are voting for. We need to consider the Trump Factor - folks don't want to appear like a racist or a bigot, so they say they don't support Trump, but in the privacy of their voting booth will most definitely vote for the man. Deep down they know that Trump is more typical than they'd like to admit. Either they're just like him or they have a buddy or family just like him. Voters will vote for him because most of them understand where he is coming from. Does he come off brash and uncouth? Absolutely, but he is more of a known than anyone is willing to admit publicly. This phenomenon is opposite of The Wilder Effect, when Virginia voters in the 1989 governor's race said that they would vote for L. Douglas Wilder because they didn't want to be considered racist, but in the end few did vote for the man, who happened to be Black. He won by a slight margin, but the polling appeared to show more support for the candidate, but the reality turns out that voters lied to save face. When most people deny they will vote for Trump, it is more to put on airs.

IN CONCLUSION

The Party Can't Stop Now, I just got here!

There is a smorgasbord of doomsdayers out there that are predicting the death of the GOP. I wholeheartedly disagree. The GOP just needs to look and act more like it did at its birth. Heck, the entire Republican Party needs to be Born Again!

As dire as things may seem now, we have faced much worse as a country (and as humanity for that matter). Just as Republicanism forged the healing of our nation at the country's darkest hour, our Civil War, so must it again before we tear this awesome country apart at the seams. Throughout its history, it has been The Republican Party that has pressed the reset button because it has found itself fluctuating between the two dueling conservative principles of equality of opportunity and protection of property, as Professor Heather Cox Richardson posits in her 2014 book, To Make Men Free: A History of the Republican Party. According to Professor Richardson, the Republican Party represents America because it rose from the moment that the country reinvented itself through the Civil War and Reconstruction. If that's the case, then it's sort of urgent that the GOP recalibrate. It's like the Republican Party mirrors

America, and we have to be forthright and honest with what we reflect. Yet, this *Come to Jesus* moment is not as difficult as it appears. All we have to do as Republicans is speak up about what it means to be one. We cannot continue to allow others to define us, especially since they do such a poor job of it. We, Republicans, ought to stay mindful of our role to this republic. No other party is responsible for conserving our republic but the Republican Party, and in order to conserve our republic, we must ensure that more people embrace our founding principles as the republic diversifies. If the Democrat Party is guilty of taking advantage of the electorate, then the Republican Party is guilty of neglecting its diversity. A year ago, I could have sworn that the GOP and conservatives were the villains in this American Tale, but even with our shortcomings, I see now that we are still the way we all prosper.

"Our future, like our past, will be what we make of it."

- Barry Goldwater

REFERENCES

Alinsky, Saul David. Rules for Radicals: A Practical Primer for Realistic Radicals. New York: Vintage, 1989. Print.

American Program: The East St. Louis Race Riot and Black Politics. By Charles L. Lumpkins. (Athens: Ohio University Press, 2008

AMA Apologizes for past Inequality against Black Doctors." - Amednews.com. American Medical News, 28 July 2008. Web. 2016.

Bell, Peter. "Public Trust in Government: 1958-2015." Pew Research Center for the People and the Press RSS. N.p., 2015. Web. 03 Nov. 2016.

Blythe, Anne, Craig Jarvis, and Jim Morrillably. "Federal Court Invalidates Maps of Two NC Congressional Districts." *Newsobserver.* N.p., 5 Feb. 2016. Web. 03 Oct. 2016.

Brewer, James H. "Robert Lee Vann, Democrat or Republican: An Exponent of Loose Leaf Politics." *Negro History Bulletin* 21:5 (1958): 101-103.

Brooks, Arthur. *The Conservative Heart: How to Build a Fairer, Happier, and More Prosperous America.* New York: Broadside Books, 2015. Print.

Buni, Andrew. *Robert L. Vann of the Pittsburgh Courier: Politics and Black Journalism.* Pittsburgh: University of Pittsburgh Press, 1974.

Butler, Shannon Moeller, Ryan Cramer, Jeff. "Howard University." What It Means to Be a Howard Law Student. N.p., n.d. Web. 2016.

"Celebrating the Life of Julian R. Dugas, a DC Trailblazer for Justice." Council for Court Excellency. N.p., n.d. Web. 28 Oct. 2016.

Decanio, Samuel. "The Compromise of 1877 and Railroad Regulation." *Democracy and the Origins of the American Regulatory State* (2015): 149-79. Web.

Dittmar, Kelly. "Reports-Status of Black Women American Politics." *Higher Heights*. N.p., n.d. Web. 29 Oct. 2016.

FairVote. "Republican Turnout Spikes in Open Primaries; Democratic Turnout Drops - IVN.us." *IVNus*. Ivn.us, 22 July 2016. Web. 29 Oct. 2016.

Farrell, Keith, TFPP Writer, C.E. Dyer, Robert Gehl, and Derrick Wilburn. "Former Senator Lieberman Blasts His Own Party Over Iran Deal." *The Federalist Papers*. N.p., 2015. Web. 03 Oct. 2016.

"Freedmen's Bureau." History.com. A&E Television Networks, 2010. Web. 21 Oct. 2016.

Free Family History and Genealogy Records - FamilySearch.org." Free Family History and Genealogy Records - FamilySearch.org. N.p., n.d. Web. 2016.

Gill, Kathy. "Equal Time - FCC Broadcasting Rules and Regulations." *About.com News & Issues*. N.p., 23 Mar. 2016. Web. 11 Oct. 2016.

Goldwater, Barry. *The Conscience of a Conservative*. Shepherdsville: Victor Publishing Company, Inc., 1960.

Griffiths, Shawn. "Large Increase in MD Unaffiliated Voters Highlights Need for Reform." *Https://ivn.us/2013/07/18/large-increase-in-md-unaffiliated-voters-highlights-need-for-reform-2/*. N.p., 18 July 2013. Web. 11 Oct. 2016.

Henderson, Nia-Malika. "Report: Black Women Are Political Powerhouse Yet Remain Socially Vulnerable." *Washington Post*. The Washington Post, 27 Mar. 2015. Web. 03 Oct 2016.

Hedrick Smith. "Issue Brief: Gerrymandering - Reclaim the American Dream." *Reclaim the American Dream*. N.p., n.d. Web. 03 Oct. 2016.

James, Professor Winston. Holding Aloft the Banner of Ethiopia, Caribbean Radicalism in Early Twentieth-Century America. N.p.: Verso, 1998. Print.

Jameson, Dennis. "George Washington's Views on Political Parties in America." *Washington Times*. The Washington Times, 31 Dec. 2014. Web. 21 Oct. 2016.

Johnson, Theodore. "The Partisan Paradox of Black Republicans." *The Atlantic*. Atlantic Media Company, 5 Feb. 2015. Web. 21 Oct. 2016.

Kemp, James, ed. *The American Idea Renewed*. Washington: Sudden Change Media, 2016. Print.

"KKK Founded." History.com. A&E Television Networks, n.d. Web. Oct. 2016.

Langer, Emily. "Julian R. Dugas, Longtime D.C. Government Leader, Dies at 95." Washington Post. The Washington Post, 14 Apr. 2014. Web. 2016.

Maloney, Brian. "Is Hillary in Trouble or Not?" Greta Slams 'racist and Shameful' Black Congressional Candidate. N.p., 2Oct. 2015. Web. 2016.

Maryland State Board of Elections. "2012 Presidential Primary Election - Statewide Voter Turnout by County and Party." *2012 Presidential Primary Election - Statewide Voter Turnout by County and Party*. N.p., n.d. Web. 21 Oct. 2016.

Montgomery 2016 Presidential Primary Election." Results. N.p., n.d. Web. 2016.

Morello, Carol. "Income Inequality Gap in D.C. One of Nation's Widest." Washington Post. The Washington Post, 2015. Web. 03 Nov. 2016.

Park, Alex, Hannah Levintova, Tasneem Raja, Ivylise Simones, and AJ Vicens, Erika Eichelberger, and Ben Dreyfuss. "The St. Louis Area Has a Long History of Shameful Racial Violence." Mother Jones. N.p., n.d. Web. Sept. 2016.

Richardson, Heather Cox. *To Make Men Free: A History of the Republican Party*. New York: Basic Books, 2014. Print.

Rigueur, Leah Wright. *The Loneliness of the Black Republican: Pragmatic Politics and the Pursuit of Power*. Princeton: Princeton UP, 2015. Print.

Robson, Seth. "US Military's Return to the Philippines Sparks Economic Hopes." Stars and Stripes. N.p., n.d. Web. 2016

Rotenstein, David. "Silver Spring, Maryland Has Whitewashed Its Past." History News Network. N.p., n.d. Web. 2016.

Russello, Gerald. "Conservatism under Academic Scrutiny." *Academic Questions* 25.1 (2012): 174-81. Web

Sitkoff, Harvard. *A New Deal for Blacks: The Emergence of Civil Rights as a National Issue: The Depression Decade*. New York: Oxford University Press, 1981.

Susskind, Jane. "Independent Voters Outnumber the Others, Why Can't They Vote." N.p., 10 Apr. 2015. Web. 11 Oct. 2016.

"Teaching History.org, Home of the National History Education Clearinghouse." East St. Louis Massacre. N.p., n.d. Web. 03 Nov. 2016

"The Black Past: Remembered and Reclaimed." East St. Louis Race Riot: July 2, 1917 | The Black Past: Remembered and Reclaimed. N.p., n.d. Web. 2016.

University of Santo Tomas." N.p., n.d. Web. 2016.

Washington, D.C., Gentrification Maps and Data. N.p., n.d. Web. 2016.

Weiner, Aaron. "D.C. Still Majority-Black, Barely." Washington City Paper. N.p., 28 June 2013. Web. 2016.

Were, Fraser. A Centennial History of Philippine Independence, 1898-1998. N.p., n.d. Web. 18 Oct. 2016.

West, Cornell. "Unmasking Black Conservatives." *Christian Century* (1986): 644. Web.

ABOUT THE AUTHOR

Liz Matory is an entrepreneur and political participant who lives in Silver Spring, Maryland. Born and raised in the District of Columbia, she is a recent graduate of the Robert H. Smith School of Business at the University of Maryland. Liz has been a non-profit fundraiser, entertainment executive, field organizer, and political candidate. *Born Again Republican* is the first publication of **Liberty Lives Media LLC**, the multi-media company that Liz established in 2016 to provide communication platforms for honest conversations.

Chante Hopkins was born on December 31, 1992 in Washington, DC and grew up in Farmville, North Carolina. She is currently finishing her Bachelor of Arts degree in Political Science at Howard University. She began working with Liz during her state delegate race in 2014. Chante served as her campaign manager for the congressional campaign.

Born Again Republican is the first book written by either author.

To connect, please send an email to BAR@LibertyLivesMedia.com.

Cover Art by Anthony Dunn.